I THE LORD AM WITH YOU ALWAYS

I The Lord Am With You Always

Prayers and Meditations for Eucharistic Adoration

Compiled by Christine McCarthy

Foreword by Most Rev. Barry Hickey, Archbishop of Perth

Nihil Obstat: Rev. Peter Joseph, S.T.D.
Imprimatur: Most Rev. Dr. George Pell,
                       Archbishop of Sydney

Date: 20 April, 2003

The Nihil Obstat and Imprimatur are a declaration that a book or pamphlet is considered to be free from doctrinal or moral error. It is not necessarily implied that those who have granted them agree with the contents, opinions or statements expressed.

Copyright © 1999 and © 2003 by Christine McCarthy
ISBN: 0-646-38156-3
    First Edition   1999
    Reprint   2001
    Second Edition   2003

Typing   Louise Kneale-Pritchard
Artwork   James McCarthy
Interior design & format   Daniel Thaine
                                Shane Phillips

Printed by McPhersons Printing Group

Proceeds from the sale of this publication support the Society for Eucharistic Adoration.

Has human language sufficient words to express what the Eucharist is?

A truly indescribable mystery!

Simple with the greatest simplicity!

Rich with supreme richness!

Pope John Paul II
Italian National Eucharistic Congress, June 1988

Dedicated in love
to the Lord Whose presence is always with us,
and to His people
that we may know, love and serve Him
more deeply.

SOCIETY FOR EUCHARISTIC ADORATION

The Society for Eucharistic Adoration is a lay organisation founded in Sydney in 1993. It seeks:

* to promote and encourage all forms of Eucharistic adoration and in particular, perpetual adoration wherever it is feasible.

* to provide a resource centre for advice and information on Eucharistic devotion and its promotion.

Membership entails:

* Spending an hour in prayer before the Blessed Sacrament once a week in any church or chapel, preferably in one's own parish church. Members pray for the Church, the intentions of the Holy Father, priests, vocations, their families, the Holy Souls in Purgatory, the sanctification of Australia and for all members of the Society.

Members can have their names registered by contacting:

The Convenor
Society for Eucharistic Adoration
142 Victoria Street
ASHFIELD NSW   2131 AUSTRALIA
Telephone: +61 2 9798 3056
Facsimile: + 61 2 9797 2273
Email: christine@mccarthys.f2s.com

Members share in the spiritual benefits of the Society. A Mass is offered each month for their spiritual and temporal welfare. Membership is free, but those who pay $5 per year are sent regular newsletters.

CONTENTS

	Foreword	10
	Introduction	11
1.	Holy Hour	13
2	Eucharistic Hymns	55
3.	Holy Mass	75
4.	Preparation for Holy Communion	99
5.	Holy Communion and Thanksgiving	123
6.	For Children	177
7.	Mary our Mother	207
8.	Priesthood and Consecrated Life	225
9.	Prayers of the People	249
10.	Perpetual Adoration	257
	Appendix of Prayers	269
	References	281

FOREWORD

This book will be a treasured resource for the growing number of people for whom Eucharistic adoration has become part of their lives. It contains a wealth of prayers, thoughts and meditations, all centred around the Real Presence of Jesus in the Blessed Sacrament.

We have been rightly reminded in the Documents of the Second Vatican Council that the Eucharist is the source and summit of the Christian Life. We should not take this to refer only to the Mass, but also to the abiding Presence of Jesus in the tabernacle, where He continues to remind us that He is the Sacrifice of the New Covenant and the Bread of Life.

Jesus calls us to know and love Him so that we might better follow Him. What better way is there to grow close to Him than in the stillness of prayer before Him in the Blessed Eucharist. Before Him in the tabernacle or exposed in the Monstrance, we spend time in His Presence, listening to Him, speaking to Him, asking to grow closer to Him.

It is a privilege for us to be able to spend time before Jesus in the Blessed Sacrament. During those precious moments we sense Jesus' tremendous love for us. We bring to Him our joys and our sorrows, we talk to Him about the needs of those around us, and we ask for that deep conversion of heart and mind that will make us one with Him.

Amid the rush and noise of the world we draw apart for a time to be quiet in mind and spirit to contemplate the great love of God for us. I commend this book to all, especially to those who have re-discovered the beauty and joy of Eucharistic adoration, and I congratulate the Society for Eucharistic Adoration for the good work it does in spreading love for our Eucharistic Lord.

Most Rev. B. J. Hickey
Archbishop of Perth

INTRODUCTION

The idea for this book came a number of years ago from a young man who is now a priest. Good ideas take time to realise, as has this one.

Originally the aim was to re-publish some ancient prayers for Eucharistic adoration. This developed further to encompass meditations, catechesis and quotations. This book is not meant to be read from cover to cover at one sitting. Here is a collage of ideas which are offered by way of stimulus to those making their Holy Hour. The focal point is the Eucharist, the Lord Who gives Himself to us in the Mass and Who remains in the tabernacle.

This is a collection of prayers ancient and modern for many occasions, prayers and thoughts to be slowly pondered. Where appropriate the beautiful language of the past has been preserved. The use of the familial, reverential "Thee/Thy" form, reserved for God and His most holy Mother, has been retained where possible. As with poetry, and long-established, traditional hymns, the language of old prayers ought not to be manipulated merely for the sake of modernity.

My deepest appreciation is offered to Fr Peter Joseph S.T.D. for the time he so generously spent correcting the final draft and giving scholarly advice. My sincerest thanks to all those members of the Society for Eucharistic Adoration who offered valuable ideas and assistance. The creativity, time and enthusiasm of my entire family have made this project more of a joy than sheer hard work.

I hope that the ideas found here will stimulate love and increase devotion for the wondrous Eucharistic presence of the Lord Who abides with us always.

Christine McCarthy

I ask that you be capable of perceiving the throbbing of the Heart of Jesus, Who invites you to an ever closer union with Him.

Pope John Paul II
Italian National Eucharistic Congress, June 1988

1

Holy Hour

Could you not watch one Hour with Me?

(Mt 26:40)

HOLY HOUR

Could you not watch one Hour with Me?

These words of Our Lord to the Apostles apply to us today. Jesus is present in the tabernacle in our churches and He wants us to visit Him, to tell Him of our joys, hopes and sufferings.

At Mass every day, Our Lord Jesus Christ renews the Sacrifice of redemption for the forgiveness of our sins and He nourishes us with Himself in Holy Communion. After Mass the Real Presence of Jesus Christ remains in the tabernacle, the proof of His great love for us.

The devotion known as the Holy Hour is public or private worship of Our Lord in the Blessed Eucharist, in the tabernacle or exposed in the monstrance.

A Holy Hour of prayer before Jesus in the Blessed Sacrament is a recognition of His wondrous presence and a channel of great graces for ourselves, for the whole Church, for the entire world. We can adore Him really present in the tabernacle or exposed in the monstrance, thank Him for His goodness, seek forgiveness for sin and ask Him for all our needs.

How lovely is Your dwelling place,
Lord, God of hosts.
My soul is longing and yearning,
is yearning for the courts of the Lord.
My heart and my soul ring out their joy
to God, the living God.

The sparrow herself finds a home
and the swallow a nest for her brood;
she lays her young by Your altars,
Lord of hosts, my king and my God.
They are happy, who dwell in Your house,
for ever singing Your praise.

They are happy, whose strength is in You,
in whose hearts are the roads to Sion.
As they go through the Bitter Valley
they make it a place of springs,
the autumn rain covers it with blessings.
They walk with ever growing strength,
they will see the God of gods in Sion.

O Lord God of hosts, hear my prayer,
give ear, O God of Jacob.
Turn Your eyes, O God, our shield,
look on the face of Your anointed.
One day within Your courts
is better than a thousand elsewhere.
The threshold of the house of God
I prefer to the dwellings of the wicked.

For the Lord God is a rampart, a shield;
He will give us His favour and glory.
The Lord will not refuse any good
to those who walk without blame.
Lord, God of hosts, happy the man who trusts in You!

Psalm 83

HOW TO MAKE THE HOLY HOUR

There is great freedom in the method of making the Holy Hour.

One may begin by making an act of faith in the presence of God. This is simplified if the eyes are focussed on the Sacred Host exposed in the monstrance or on the Lord reserved in the tabernacle.

In our own words, the words of the Psalms, the Scriptures, the Divine Office and many of the great hymns, we adore Our Lord, we ask for pardon, we petition Him for our parish, the Church, for vocations, for the world, we thank Him for all that He has given us.

We are advised to talk silently to Our Lord, but also to listen. It is in silence that we know God: *"Be still and know that I am God."* (Ps 45:11).

One day within Your courts is better than a thousand elsewhere.
(Ps 83:11)

A VISIT TO THE BLESSED SACRAMENT

My Lord Jesus Christ Who, for the love which Thou bearest to men, remainest night and day in this Sacrament full of compassion and of love, awaiting, calling, and welcoming all who come to visit Thee, I believe that Thou art present in the Sacrament of the Altar.

I adore Thee from the abyss of my nothingness and I thank Thee for all the graces which Thou hast bestowed upon me, and in particular for having given me Thyself in this Sacrament.

My Jesus, I love Thee with my whole heart. I grieve for having hitherto so many times offended Thy infinite goodness. I purpose by Thy grace never more to offend Thee.

I consecrate myself to Thee without reserve. I give Thee and renounce my entire will, my affections, my desires, and all that I possess. Dispose of me and of all that I have as Thou pleasest. All that I ask of Thee and desire is Thy holy love, final perseverance, and the perfect accomplishment of Thy will.

I recommend to Thee the souls of purgatory but especially those who had the greatest devotion to the Most Blessed Sacrament and to the Most Blessed Virgin Mary. I also recommend to Thee all poor sinners.

My dear Saviour, I unite all my affections with the affections of Thy most loving Heart and I offer them, thus united, to Thy Eternal Father.

St Alphonsus Liguori
The Holy Eucharist

DIALOGUE

This hour is simply a period of conversation between the individual soul and God Himself. Whatever form that dialogue takes is under the guidance of the Holy Spirit Who inspires and directs all our prayers. We, for our part, might find it useful to keep a few points in mind. The presence of Our Lord in the Blessed Sacrament is derived from the Sacrifice of Calvary, made present at the Consecration at every Mass.

The four ends of the Mass are the same as the four ends of prayer: to adore God, to thank Him, to make reparation for sin, and to petition Him for all our needs. In a very real sense, prayer before the Blessed Sacrament perpetuates these four ends of the Sacrifice of the Mass.

Initially it is useful to make an act of faith in Our Lord truly present. This concentrates and focuses the mind on the One to Whom we pray. As in prayer, so in posture, there is flexibility. We can kneel, sit, or stand depending on our tradition and our preference as to what is the most prayerful and least distracting posture.

Enter His courts with songs of praise. (Ps 99:4)

A SHORT VISIT TO THE BLESSED SACRAMENT BEFORE MEDITATION

I place myself in the presence of Him, in Whose Incarnate Presence I am before I place myself there.

I adore Thee, O my Saviour, present here as God and man, in soul and body, in true flesh and blood.

I acknowledge and confess that I kneel before that Sacred Humanity, which was conceived in Mary's womb, and lay in Mary's bosom; which grew up to man's estate, and by the Sea of Galilee called the Twelve, wrought miracles, and spoke words of wisdom and peace; which in due season hung on the cross, lay in the tomb, rose from the dead, and now reigns in heaven.

I praise, and bless, and give myself wholly to Him, Who is the true Bread of my soul, and my everlasting joy.

Cardinal Newman
Meditations and Devotions

ACT OF FAITH

My Jesus, I firmly believe that Thou art really and truly present here, God and Man, in the Sacrament of Thy Love, because Thou hast said it and Thy Word is true.
My Lord and My God!

Bishop Ryan
Eucharistic Hours

ADORATION

Adoration is the highest form of prayer whereby we give honour to the Triune God and acknowledge Him as our Creator, Redeemer and Sanctifier. Adoration is always the prime act in any sacrifice and it is a very important part of our prayer before and after Mass. Adoration encompasses acts of love, acknowledgement of God as our Creator, of His great goodness in remaining forever with us under the Eucharistic species.

THANKSGIVING

We could spend some time dwelling on the great treasure to be found in the Blessed Sacrament, then perhaps move on to the second aim of prayer, thanksgiving, whereby we thank God for all His graces, for the beauty and grandeur of the world He has created, for all the good things we have and for the people we love. We might thank God, particularly, for His presence in the Blessed Sacrament and tell Him of our profound joy and pleasure at being in His company.

They are happy who dwell in Your house. (Ps 83:5)

ACTS OF ADORATION AND GRATITUDE

O my God, I firmly believe that Thou art really and corporally present in the Blessed Sacrament of the altar. I adore Thee here present from the very depths of my heart, and I worship Thy sacred presence with all possible humility. O my soul, what joy to have Jesus Christ always with us, and to be able to speak to Him, heart to heart, with all confidence. Grant, O Lord, that I, having adored Thy divine Majesty here on earth in this wonderful Sacrament, may be able to adore It eternally in heaven.

Amen.

The Raccolta

I adore Thee, O Jesus, true God and true Man, here present in the Holy Eucharist, humbly kneeling before Thee and united in spirit with all the faithful on earth and all the blessed in heaven. In deepest gratitude for so great a blessing, I love Thee, my Jesus, with my whole heart, for Thou art all perfect and all worthy of love.

Give me grace nevermore in any way to offend Thee, and grant that I, being refreshed by Thy Eucharistic presence here on earth, may be found worthy to come to the enjoyment with Mary of Thine eternal and ever-blessed presence in heaven.

Amen.

Ibid

REPARATION

The third end of prayer is reparation for our own sins and for those of the world. We can, united with the crucified Christ, atone for the indifference and coldness which He frequently receives. His Eucharistic presence is our greatest grace and His continual presence in the tabernacle after Mass is our central belief as Catholics. So often He is treated with irreverence or ignored. Our weekly hour can be offered to God to atone for such ingratitude and insensitivity.

PETITION

The fourth end of prayer is petition. We have many petitions to make to Our Lord - for the Church, the intentions of the Holy Father, priests, vocations, the Holy Souls in purgatory, the sanctification of our families and our nation.

Out of the depths I cry to You, O Lord . (Ps 129:1)

AN ACT OF ADORATION AND REPARATION

I adore Thee profoundly, O my Jesus, in Thy sacramental form; I acknowledge Thee to be true God and true Man, and by this act of adoration I intend to atone for the coldness of so many Christians who pass before Thy churches and sometimes before the very Tabernacle in which Thou art pleased to remain at all hours with loving impatience to give Thyself to Thy faithful people, and do not so much as bend the knee before Thee, and who, by their indifference proclaim that they grow weary of this heavenly manna, like the people of Israel in the wilderness.

I offer Thee, in reparation for this grievous negligence, the Precious Blood which Thou didst shed from Thy five wounds, and especially from Thy sacred Side, and entering therein, I repeat a thousand times with true recollection of spirit:

O Sacrament most holy!

O Sacrament Divine!

All praise and all thanksgiving
be every moment Thine.

The Raccolta

SPIRITUAL BOOKS

It may be helpful to use a passage from the Scriptures, particularly a verse or two from the Psalms or some spiritual book as the subject for our conversation with Our Lord. Some people find it useful to take Our Lord's own prayer, the Our Father, and dwell on each individual phrase, in turn, in His presence. Others may find the Magnificat or the last seven words of Our Lord on the Cross useful material for prayer.

PERSONAL PRAYER HELPS THE CHURCH

It is impossible to measure the spiritual benefits and graces granted to those who spend time in the presence of Our Lord in the Blessed Sacrament. As members of the Church, the Mystical Body of Christ, our actions and prayers bear fruit. Every devout reception of Communion, every good Confession and every prayer has positive ramifications for the whole Church.

Personal growth in the spiritual life is an apostolic activity. Silent prayer should, then, always be seen in the context of the universal Church. Our prayer helps the whole Church.

Praise is fitting for loyal hearts. (Ps 32:1)

PRAYER OF PRAISE

Thou art Christ, my holy Father, my tender God, my great King, my good Shepherd, my one Master, my best Helper, my most Beautiful and my Beloved, my living Bread, my Priest forever, my Leader to my country, my true Light, my holy Sweetness, my straight Way, my excellent Wisdom, my pure Simplicity, my pacific Harmony, my whole Guard, my good Portion, my everlasting Salvation.

Christ Jesus, my sweet Lord, why have I ever loved, why in my whole life have I ever desired anything except Thee, Jesus my God? Where was I when I was not in Thy mind with Thee? Now, from this time forth, do ye, all my desires, grow hot, and flow out upon the Lord Jesus; run, ye have been tardy thus far; hasten whither ye are going; seek Whom ye are seeking. O Jesus, may he who loves Thee not, be anathema; may he who loves Thee not, be filled with bitterness!

O sweet Jesus, may every good feeling that is fitted for Thy praise, love Thee, delight in Thee, admire Thee. God of my heart and my Portion, Christ Jesus, may my heart faint away in spirit and mayest Thou be my life within me! May the life of Thy love grow hot within my spirit, and break forth into a perfect fire; may it burn incessantly on the altar of my heart; may it glow in my innermost being; may it blaze in hidden recesses of my soul; and in the day of my consummation, may I be found consummated with Thee.

Amen.

St Augustine of Hippo

HIS REAL PRESENCE

The visit to the Blessed Sacrament is a great treasure of the Catholic faith. It nourishes social love and gives us opportunities for adoration and thanksgiving, for reparation and supplication. Benediction of the Blessed Sacrament, Exposition and Adoration of the Blessed Sacrament, Holy Hours and Eucharistic processions are likewise precious elements of your heritage - in full accord with the teaching of the Second Vatican Council.

Every act of reverence, every genuflection that you make before the Blessed Sacrament, is important because it is an act of faith in Christ, an act of love for Christ. And every sign of the Cross and gesture of respect made each time you pass a church is also an act of faith. May God preserve you in this faith - this holy Catholic faith - this faith in the Blessed Sacrament.

Pope John Paul II
Phoenix Park, Ireland, 1979

SACRIFICE, PRESENCE, BANQUET

The mystery of the Eucharist - sacrifice, presence, banquet - does not allow for reduction or exploitation; it must be experienced and lived in its integrity, both in its celebration and in the intimate converse with Jesus which takes place after receiving communion or in a prayerful moment of Eucharistic adoration apart from Mass. These are times when the Church is firmly built up and it becomes clear what she truly is: one, holy, catholic and apostolic; the people, temple and family of God; the body and bride of Christ, enlivened by the Holy Spirit; the universal sacrament of salvation and a hierarchically structured communion.

Pope John Paul II
Ecclesia de Eucharistia, **2003**

*He who eats My Flesh and drinks My Blood
lives in Me and I live in him.* (Jn 6: 56)

JESUS CHRIST, THE ONLY SAVIOUR OF THE WORLD, BREAD FOR NEW LIFE

Exposition of the Blessed Sacrament, hours of adoration, Eucharistic processions, especially on the solemn feast of Corpus Christi, and Eucharistic congresses concentrate our attention on the One who is the Bread of life, life itself. They remind and give witness to all that man does not live by bread alone.

In the Virgin's example of silent and fruitful listening, contemplation helps grasp the presence of the Living One in the Eucharist and aids in transfiguring the deaths that mark the earthly city into a commitment for life and hope in the resurrection.

**Pope John Paul II
47th International Eucharistic Congress,
June 2000**

WORSHIP OF THE EUCHARIST

In the liturgy of the Mass we express our faith in the Real Presence of Christ under the species of bread and wine by, among other ways, genuflecting or bowing deeply as a sign of adoration of the Lord. "The Catholic Church has always offered and still offers to the sacrament of the Eucharist the cult of adoration, not only during Mass, but also outside of it, reserving the consecrated hosts with the utmost care, exposing them to the solemn veneration of the faithful, and carrying them in procession."[1]

**Catechism of the Catholic Church
Para 1378**

---

1. Pope Paul VI, *Mysterium Fidei 56*.

BEFORE THE TABERNACLE

Pause before the tabernacle by yourself, for no special reason, even without saying a thing, simply remaining in His presence, contemplating the supreme gestures of love contained in the consecrated Bread. Learn to remain with Him, to be able to love like Him. When you can, during the week, take part in Holy Mass. Fidelity to the weekday Eucharist helps us to follow Christ in daily life, and gives us light and strength as we follow our vocation.

Look to Mary! She welcomed the infinite mystery of the love of the Triune God in her person and in her life. Mary lived as a continuous Eucharist: she always remained intimately bound to Jesus and followed Him faithfully from the time when He was incarnate in her virginal womb until Calvary.

Pope John Paul II
Trent, April 1995

IN SILENT ADORATION

It is pleasant to spend time with Him, to lie close to His breast like the Beloved Disciple (cf. Jn 13:25) and to feel the infinite love present in His heart. If in our time Christians must be distinguished above all by the "art of prayer"[1], how can we not feel a renewed need to spend time in spiritual converse, in silent adoration, in heartfelt love before Christ present in the Most Holy Sacrament? How often, dear brothers and sisters, have I experienced this, and drawn from it strength, consolation and support!

Pope John Paul II
Ecclesia de Eucharistia, **2003**

1. John Paul II, Apostolic Letter *Novo Millennio Ineunte*, 2001.

My happiness lies in You alone. (Ps 15:22)

SOURCE AND SUMMIT OF THE CHRISTIAN LIFE

The Eucharist is "the source and summit of the Christian life".[1] "The other sacraments, and indeed all ecclesiastical ministries and works of the apostolate, are bound up with the Eucharist and are oriented toward it. For in the Blessed Eucharist is contained the whole spiritual good of the Church, namely Christ Himself, our Pasch."[2]

Catechism of the Catholic Church
Para 1324

1. *Lumen Gentium 11*
2. *Presbyterorum Ordinis 5*

PRAYER FOR EUCHARISTIC CONGRESSES

O Jesus, who are really, truly and substantially present in the Blessed Sacrament to be the food of our souls, deign to bless and bring to a successful issue all Eucharistic congresses and gatherings, and especially the coming congress in ...

Be Thou the inspiration of their labours, resolutions and vows; accept graciously the solemn homage there rendered to Thee; enkindle the hearts of priests and faithful, of parents and children, so that frequent and daily Communion may be held in honour in all the countries of the world; and grant that the Kingship of the Sacred Heart over human society may everywhere be acknowledged. Sacred Heart of Jesus, bless the Congress. Saint Paschal Baylon, pray for us.

The Raccolta

THE TABERNACLE, OUR BETHANY

Jesus hides in the Blessed Sacrament of the altar because He wants us to *dare* to approach Him.

When we meet together around the altar to celebrate the holy sacrifice of the Mass, when we contemplate the sacred host in the monstrance or adore Him hidden in the tabernacle, our faith should be strengthened; we should reflect on this new life which we are receiving and be moved by God's affection and tenderness.

For me the tabernacle has always been a Bethany, a quiet and pleasant place where Christ resides, a place where we can tell Him about our worries, our sufferings, our desires, our joys, with the same sort of simplicity and naturalness as Martha, Mary and Lazarus. That is why I rejoice when I stumble upon a church in town or in the country; it's another tabernacle, another opportunity for the soul to escape and join in intention our Lord in the Sacrament.

St Josemaría Escrivá de Balaguer
Christ is Passing By

Come in, let us bow and bend low. (Ps 94:6)

JESUS IN THE TABERNACLE

What happiness do we not feel in the Presence of God, when we are alone at His feet before the Sacred Tabernacle! Redouble your fervour; you are alone to adore your God; His eyes rest upon you alone.

St John Vianney
Catechism on the Real Presence

I find my consolation in my one Companion Who never abandons me.

Blessed Damien de Veuster
the Apostle of Molokai
when speaking of Christ's Real Presence in the tabernacle

Reprinted from L'Osservatore Romano English edition

When you approach the tabernacle, remember that He has been waiting for you for twenty centuries.

St Josemaría Escrivá de Balaguer
The Way 537

MY LONGINGS BEFORE JESUS
HIDDEN IN HIS PRISON OF LOVE

O happy key, since you exist
For this: you open, every day,
The prison of the Eucharist.
The God of Love is locked away!
But I can turn the mortice (for
My faith can do this wondrous thing),
Can open up the golden door,
To hide, beside my Heav'nly King.

I'd like to burn away, to be
Consumed - near God by day and night;
A steady glow of mystery,
A sanctuary lamp, alight.
What happiness is mine: I've flame
Within me! ... Daily thus can I
Win Jesus *souls*, and by the same
Heart's-fire He came to light them by.

O Sacred Altar-stone, you fill
Me, every dawn, with envy too,
As the Eternal, by His Will -
A Bethlehem - is born on You.
Then, enter in this soul (my Own,
My Saviour!), since for You it burns:
Far from the coldness of a stone,
It's *that* for which Your own Heart yearns.

O Altar-cloth! where angels go-
How, too, I envy you in this:
I see my Jesus ... there, as though
In swaddling-clothes, my Treasure is!
Change my heart, Mary! so I am
An Altar-cloth that's pure and bright,
Then may my heart receive your Lamb
Who hides Himself ... the Host of white.

Paten, I envy you as well! -
Upon you Jesus takes His rest;
May Endless Grandeur come and dwell
(Though poor the lodging) as my Guest! ...
He's here with me - He doesn't wait
Until the dusk of life I see:
He comes, and - how my joy is great! -
A living Monstrance makes of me.

And how I envy you your prize -
The Blood of God, O happy Cup!
But I, too, at the Sacrifice,
Those precious drops can gather up.
Much dearer Jesus values me
Than golden vessels, jewel-set:
The Altar a new Calvary,
His Blood for me is flowing yet.

I am (O Jesus, Holy Vine,
To whom our fruitfulness is due)
A bunch of grapes - O King Divine! -
That ought to disappear for You.
It's in the Winepress - Suffering -
That I'll be proving what I say:
The joy of love to which I cling
Is self-oblation, every day!

That I should have been chosen there
Among the grains of purest Wheat,
That I may in their dying share,
For Jesus: thus my joy's complete!
I am Your spouse: You'll always be
My Love - come live in me! I say:
O come ... You have enraptured me -
Transform me into You, I pray!

St Thérèse of Lisieux
Collected Poems of St Thérèse of Lisieux
(Gracewing, England)
Translated by Alan Bancroft

LOVE AND PRAYER

Look with trust to Christ; renew your love for Him present in the Eucharistic Sacrament. He is the divine Guest of the soul, the support for every weakness, the strength for every trial, the consolation for every sorrow, the Bread of life, the supreme destiny of every human being .

From the countless tabernacles scattered about the country gleams the light of that truth and the warmth of that love which contains the hope of the future for this people, as for every other people of the world.

Pope John Paul II
Closing Mass
Italian National Eucharistic Congress
Bologna, June 1997

PRICELESS TREASURE

The Eucharist is a priceless treasure: by not only celebrating it but also by praying before it outside of Mass we are enabled to make contact with the very wellspring of grace. A Christian community desirous of contemplating the face of Christ cannot fail also to develop this aspect of Eucharistic worship, which prolongs and increases the fruits of our communion in the body and blood of the Lord.

Pope John Paul II
Ecclesia de Eucharistia, **2003**

O God, You are my God, for You I long. (Ps 62:1)

HYMN OF PRAISE

Blessed are You, O Lord, the God of our fathers,
praiseworthy and exalted above all forever;

And blessed is Your holy and glorious name,
praiseworthy and exalted above all for all ages.

Blessed are You in the temple of Your holy glory,
praiseworthy and glorious above all forever.

Blessed are You on the throne of Your kingdom,
praiseworthy and exalted above all forever.

Blessed are You who look into the depths
from Your throne upon the cherubim,
praiseworthy and exalted above all forever.

Blessed are You in the firmament of heaven,
praiseworthy and glorious forever.

Bless the Lord, all you works of the Lord,
praise and exalt Him above all forever.
Angels of the Lord, bless the Lord,
praise and exalt Him above all forever.

You heavens, bless the Lord,
praise and exalt Him above all forever.

(Dan 3:52-57)

PRAYER AND ACTION

Action presupposes contemplation: it springs from the latter and is nourished by it. Love cannot be given to one's brothers and sisters unless it has first been drawn from the genuine source of divine charity, and this happens only in prolonged moments of prayer, of listening to the Word of God, of adoring the Eucharist, the source and summit of the Christian life. Prayer and active involvement form a vital, inseparable and fruitful combination.

Pope John Paul II
Mass for Day of Charity
Rome, May 1999

THE EUCHARIST OUR STRENGTH

Every commitment to holiness, every activity aimed at carrying out the Church's mission, every work of pastoral planning, must draw the strength it needs from the Eucharistic mystery and in turn be directed to that mystery as its culmination. In the Eucharist we have Jesus, we have His redemptive sacrifice, we have His resurrection, we have the gift of the Holy Spirit, we have adoration, obedience and love of the Father. Were we to disregard the Eucharist, how could we overcome our own deficiency?

Pope John Paul II
***Ecclesia de Eucharistia*, 2003**

For You my soul is thirsting. (Ps 62:2)

PSALM 62

O God, You are my God, for You I long;
for You my soul is thirsting.
My body pines for You
like a dry, weary land without water.
So I gaze on You in the sanctuary
to see Your strength and Your glory.

For Your love is better than life,
my lips will speak Your praise.
So I will bless You all my life,
in Your Name I will lift up my hands.
My soul shall be filled as with a banquet,
my mouth shall praise You with joy.

On my bed I remember You.
On You I muse through the night
for You have been my help;
in the shadow of Your wings I rejoice.
My soul clings to You;
Your right hand holds me fast.

Those who seek to destroy my life
shall go down to the depths of the earth.
They shall be put into the power of the sword
and left as the prey of the jackals.
But the king shall rejoice in God;
(all that swear by Him shall be blessed)
for the mouth of liars shall be silenced.

WORSHIP OF THE BLESSED SACRAMENT

When the faithful worship Christ in the Blessed Sacrament they should recollect that this presence is derived from the Sacrifice and evokes sacramental and spiritual communion.

That piety, therefore, which moves the faithful to adore the Blessed Sacrament inspires them also to participate more fully in the paschal mystery and to respond with grateful hearts to Christ's gift of Himself, Who through His humanity is ever bestowing divine life on the members of His mystical body.

Remaining closely united to Christ, they enjoy intimate familiarity with Him and offer heart-felt prayer to Him for themselves, for all those who are dear to them, for peace and for the salvation of the world, offering their entire lives with Christ to the Father in the Holy Spirit.

From this admirable exchange they receive an increase of hope and charity. In this way they develop the right dispositions for celebrating the memorial of the Lord with fitting devotion and for receiving frequently the heavenly Bread which the Father has provided for us.

The faithful should, therefore, be zealous, in keeping with their conditions of life, in their devotion to the Blessed Sacrament.

Eucharistiae Sacramentum
Sacred Congregation for Divine Worship, 1973

I gaze on You in the sanctuary
to see Your strength and Your glory. (Ps 62:3)

TO THE LORD WHO DWELLS WITH US

Glory be to Thee, O Jesus, King and Spouse, Whom my soul loveth. Thou hast given me for my food the Living Bread. Thou art dwelling in me.

I praise Thee and thank Thee, O Thou lover of souls, as Thou dwellest in the tabernacle. I praise Thee and thank Thee, as Thou dwellest in the souls of all who have received Thee worthily this day, wherever they may be. I praise Thee and love Thee for giving Thyself to the unworthy, who gave no welcome to Thee. I hope and pray, dear Jesus, that Thou art dwelling in my soul and filling it with grace.

Thou drivest the darkness from me and makest me glad. Thou art light to me in every danger and strength in every weakness. Thou art my comfort in all sorrow and my rest in all weariness and pain. Thou art the healer of every woe.

Thy voice, O Thou Beloved of the Father, is in my heart like the song of the morning stars.

Keep me faithful, Thou Lord of life and love, that I may rejoice with the sons of God.

Anon

HE DWELLS WITHIN US

Let us therefore do all things in the conviction that He dwells in us. Thus we shall be His temples and He will be our God within us. This is the truth, and it will be made manifest before our eyes. Let us, then, love Him as He deserves.

St Ignatius of Antioch

If the soul is put in regular, daily contact with Our Lord, His charm will soon have its influence.

Eugene Boylan
This Tremendous Lover

The man who has been wounded by the love of Christ is lovingly open to every man.

Dietrich von Hildebrand
Liturgy and Personality

All interior life needs silence and intimacy with Christ in order to develop.

Pope John Paul II
Belgium, 1996

Your love is better than life. (Ps 62:4)

ACT OF DIVINE LOVE

O my sweet Spouse! my dear Lord Jesus! draw to Thyself all the power of my soul; inflame and animate my heart with Thy most pure and ardent love. I ask of Thee, Lord, no earthly treasure, no worldly goods or glory. I beg only the riches of Thy pure love, that in all things I may seek Thee alone, prize Thee alone, be content with Thee alone, Who art my all.

O love of my God! the life of my soul, the centre of all my actions, to Thee I dedicate unreservedly all my desires, all my labours, all I am, and all I have; in fine, my whole being. May I not live one moment, but to love Thee, my God; may I not even breathe but to glorify Thee!

O that I could break forth without intermission into seraphic acts of love! O that I could continue to repeat them each moment of my life! O my divine Spouse, may I die in the highest and most perfect exercise of divine love, that I may love and glorify Thee for a blessed eternity.

Amen.

Anon

FRIENDSHIP WITH JESUS

What can the world profit thee without Jesus?

To be without Jesus is a grievous hell, and to be with Jesus a sweet paradise.

If Jesus be with thee, no enemy can hurt thee.

Whosoever findeth Jesus findeth a good treasure, yes, good above all goods.

And he that loseth Jesus loseth exceeding much, and more than if he lost the whole world.

He is wretchedly poor who liveth without Jesus; and he is exceedingly rich, who is well with Jesus.

We should rather choose to have the whole world against us than to offend Jesus.

Of all therefore, that are dear to thee, let Jesus always be thy special beloved.

Thomas à Kempis
***The Imitation of Christ* (II: 8, 2)**

Open to me the gates of holiness. (Ps 117:19)

OUR THIRST FOR JESUS

O most sweet Lord Jesus Christ, transfix the affections of my inmost soul with the most joyous and healthful wound of Thy love, with true, serene, holiest apostolic charity, that my soul may ever languish and melt with entire love and longing for Thee, that it may desire Thee, and faint for Thy court, long to be dissolved and to be with Thee.

Grant that my soul may hunger after Thee, the Bread of Angels, the Refreshment of holy souls, our daily and supersubstantial Bread, Who hast all sweetness and savour, and the delight of every taste. Let my heart ever hunger after and feed upon Thee, upon Whom the Angels desire to look and my inmost soul be filled with the sweetness of Thy savour. May it ever thirst for Thee, the Fountain of life, the Source of wisdom and knowledge, the Fountain of eternal light, the Torrent of pleasure, the Richness of the House of God.

May it ever yearn for Thee, seek Thee, find Thee, stretch towards Thee, attain to Thee, meditate upon Thee, speak of Thee, and do all things to the praise and glory of Thy holy name, with humility and discretion, with love and delight, with readiness and affection, with perseverance even unto the end.

Be Thou ever my hope and my whole confidence, my riches, my delight, my pleasure and my joy, my rest and tranquility, my peace, my sweetness, and my fragrance, my sweet savour, my food and refreshment, my refuge and my help, my wisdom, my portion, my possession, and my treasure, in Whom my mind and my heart may ever remain fixed and firm, and rooted immovably, henceforth and for evermore,

Amen.

St Bonaventure

PRAYER TO THE SUFFERING CHRIST

I fall in adoration at Your feet, Lord!
I thank You, God of goodness;
God of holiness, I invoke You,
on my knees, in Your sight ...

For me, an unworthy sinner,
You have willed to undergo
the death of the cross,
setting me free from the bonds of evil.

What shall I offer You in return for
Your generosity?

Glory to You, friend of men!
Glory to You, most merciful!
Glory to You, most patient!
Glory to You who forgive sin!
Glory to You who have come to save us!
Glory to You who have been made man
in the womb of a Virgin!

Glory to You who have been bound!
Glory to You who have been scourged!
Glory to You who have been derided!
Glory to You who have been nailed to the cross!
Glory to You, laid in the sepulchre,
but risen again!

Glory to You who have preached the Gospel to men
and have been believed!
Glory to You who have ascended to heaven!

Glory to You, seated at the right hand
of the Father and who will return with Him,
in majesty, among the angels, to judge
those who have disregarded Your passion!

The powers of heaven will be shaken;
all the angels and archangels,
the cherubim and seraphim
will appear in fear and trembling
before Your glory;
the foundations of the earth will quake
and all that has life will cry out
before Your majesty.

In that hour let Your hand draw me
beneath Your wings,
and save me from the terrible fire,
from the gnashing of teeth,
from the outer darkness and
from despair without end.
That I may sing to Your glory:
glory to Him who through
His merciful goodness
has deigned to redeem the sinner.

**St Ephrem of Syria
in *Hymns to Christ***

OUR OFFERING

Closely united with Christ, then, we all seek to immerse ourselves in His holy soul and to make ourselves one with Him, that we may have our part in these acts of pleasing and acceptable homage which He pays to the Blessed Trinity; those acts of supreme praise and thanksgiving which He offers to the Eternal Father, and with which heaven and earth join in harmonious song, according to the words: *"Bless the Lord, all ye works of the Lord"*, acts by which, above all, we offer and immolate ourselves as victims, saying: *"Make us an eternal offering to Thee."*

Pope Pius XII
Mediator Dei, **1947**

There is no oblation more worthy, nor satisfaction greater for the washing away of sins, than to offer up thyself purely and entirely to God, together with the oblation of the Body of Christ, in the Mass and in Communion.

Thomas à Kempis
The Imitation of Christ **(IV: 7, 4)**

To You, O Lord, I lift up my soul. (Ps 24:1)

FATIMA PRAYERS

My God, I believe in You, I hope in You, I adore You, I love You. I ask pardon of You for all those who do not believe in You, do not hope in You, do not adore You, do not love You.

Most Holy Trinity, Father, Son and Holy Spirit, I adore You profoundly. I offer You the most Precious Body, Blood, Soul and Divinity of Jesus Christ, present in all the tabernacles of the world in reparation for the outrages, sacrileges and indifference, by which He Himself is offended. By the infinite merits of the most Sacred Heart of Jesus and through the Immaculate Heart of Mary, I beg of You the conversion of poor sinners.

**Given by the Angel
to the children at Fatima, 1916**

ON EXPOSITION

When you see (the Body of Christ) exposed, say to yourself: It is on account of this Body that I am no longer earth and ashes, no longer captive, but free.

This Body gives me my hope of heaven and the treasures there laid up for me: life without end, the company of the angels, familiar intercourse with Christ.

This Body was pierced by the nails, torn with scourges, yet death has not taken it from me; this is the very Body that was drenched with blood, pierced by the lance; the Body from which two springs of salvation gushed forth, one of blood and one of water.

This Body He has given us to hold and to eat - a proof of His ardent love.

St John Chrysostom
quoted in *Mediator Dei*
Pope Pius XII, 1947

HIS PRESENCE AMONG US

In the humble signs of bread and wine, changed into His body and blood, Christ walks beside us as our strength and our food for the journey, and He enables us to become, for everyone, witnesses of hope. If, in the presence of this mystery, reason experiences its limits, the heart, enlightened by the grace of the Holy Spirit, clearly sees the response that is demanded, and bows low in adoration and unbounded love.

Pope John Paul II
***Ecclesia de Eucharistia*, 2003**

He is your Lord, pay homage to Him. (Ps 44:12)

THROUGH HIM, WITH HIM, IN HIM

O my soul, you must go into the very heart of the Adorable Trinity and contemplate there the eternal Liturgy in which the three Persons chant, one to another, their divine Life and infinite Sanctity, in their ineffable hymn of the generation of the Word and the procession of the Holy Spirit. *Sicut erat in principio ...*[1]

God desires to be praised outside of Himself. He created the angels, and heaven resounded with their joyous cries of *Sanctus, Sanctus, Sanctus.* He created the visible world and it magnified His power: "The heavens announce the glory of God."

You, Jesus, You alone are the perfect hymn of praise, because You are the true glory of the Father. No one can worthily glorify Your Father, except through You. *Per Ipsum, et cum Ipso et in Ipso est tibi Deo Patri ... omnis honor et gloria.*[2]

You are the link between the Liturgy of earth and the Liturgy of heaven, in which You give Your elect a more direct participation. Your Incarnation came and united, in a living and substantial union, mankind and all creation, with the Liturgy of God Himself. Thus it is God Who praises God, in our Liturgy. And this is full and perfect praise, which finds its apogee in the sacrifice of Calvary.

Dom Chautard
The Soul of the Apostolate

1. As it was in the beginning ...

2. Through Him and with Him and in Him, all honour and glory is given to Thee, O God the Father. (Canon of the Mass)

THE MIRACLE OF THE EUCHARIST

Jesus Christ, perfect God and perfect man, leaves us, not a symbol, but a reality. He Himself stays with us. He will go to the Father, but He will also remain among men. He will leave us, not simply a gift that will make us remember Him, not an image that becomes blurred with time, like a photograph that soon fades and yellows, and has no meaning except for those who were contemporaries.

Under the appearances of bread and wine, He is really present with His Body and Blood, with His soul and divinity.

The miracle of the holy Eucharist is being continually renewed and it has all Jesus' personal traits. Perfect God and perfect man, Lord of heaven and earth, He offers Himself to us as nourishment in the most natural and ordinary way.

Love has been awaiting us for almost two thousand years. That's a long time and yet it's not, for when you are in love time flies.

St Josemaría Escrivá de Balaguer
Christ is Passing By

I will be their God, they shall be My people. (Ez 37:27)

HOLY SONNET

Batter my heart, three-personed God, for You
As yet but knock, breathe, shine, and seek to mend;
That I may rise and stand, o'erthrow me and bend
Your force to break, blow, burn, and make me new.
I, like an usurped town to another due,
Labour to admit You, but O, to no end.
Reason, Your viceroy in me, me should defend,
But is captive and proves weak or untrue.

Yet dearly I love You and would be loved fain,
But am betrothed unto Your enemy.
Divorce me, untie, or break that knot again,
Take me to You, imprison me, for I,
Except You enthrall me, never shall be free,
Nor ever chaste except You ravish me.

John Donne

BE THOU MY VISION

Be Thou my vision, O Lord of my heart,
Naught be all else to me, save that Thou art;
Thou my best thought in the day and the night,
Waking or sleeping, Thy presence my light.

Be Thou my wisdom, be Thou my true word,
I ever with Thee, and Thou with me, Lord;
Thou my great Father, and I Thy true son;
Thou in me dwelling, and I with Thee one.

Riches I heed not, nor man's empty praise,
Thou mine inheritance through all my days;
Thou, and Thou only the first in my heart,
High King of heaven, my treasure Thou art!

High King of heaven, Thou heaven's bright sun,
Grant me its joys after vict'ry is won;
Christ of my own heart, whatever befall,
Still be my vision, O Ruler of all.

Eleanor Henrietta Hull

From the rising of the sun to its setting
Praised be the name of the Lord! (Ps 112:3)

GOD'S GRANDEUR

The world is charged with the grandeur of God.
It will flame out, like shining from shook foil;
It gathers to a greatness, like the ooze of oil
Crushed. Why do men then now not reck His rod?
Generations have trod, have trod, have trod;
And all is seared with trade; bleared, smeared with toil;
And wears man's smudge and shares man's smell:
the soil
Is bare now, nor can foot feel, being shod.

And for all this, nature is never spent;
There lives the dearest freshness deep down things;
And though the last lights off the black West went
Oh, morning, at the brown brink eastward, springs–
Because the Holy Ghost over the bent
World broods with warm breast and with ah!
bright wings.

Gerard Manley Hopkins SJ

THE MAGNET OF SOULS

The Blessed Sacrament is the magnet of souls. There is a mutual attraction between Jesus and the souls of men.

Mary drew Him down from heaven. Our nature attracted Him rather than the nature of angels. Our misery caused Him to stoop to our lowness.

Even our sins had a sort of attraction for the abundance of His mercy and the predilection of His grace. Our repentance wins Him to us.

Our love makes earth a paradise to Him; and our souls lure Him as gold lures the miser, with irresistible fascination.

He draws us to Himself by grace, by example, by power, by lovingness, by beauty, by pardon, and above all by the Blessed Sacrament.

Frederick Faber
The Blessed Sacrament

2

Eucharistic Hymns

*O sing to the Lord;
Make music to His name*

(Ps 67:5)

Sing a new song to the Lord. (Ps 149:1)

TRADITIONAL SONG

Hail Body of Jesus, consecrated on the altar

Hail Body of Jesus, conceived by the Holy Spirit

Hail Body of Jesus, born of the Virgin

Hail Body of Jesus, placed in a manger

Hail Body of Jesus, so greatly tortured

Hail Body of Jesus, nailed to the cross for us

Hail Body of Jesus, buried in a tomb

Hail Body of Jesus, risen on the third day

Hail Body of Jesus, ascended to Heaven

Hail Body of Jesus, glorified throughout the world

Hail Body of Jesus, given to all for our food

Hail Bread, sweeter than honey, food of faithful souls

Hail Trinity in unity, hail Jesus in divinity

Yours be the thanks, the praise, the glory most great.

O Jesus, be praised for ever and ever.

Amen

Kastav, Istra (Croatia)

O SALUTARIS HOSTIA

O Salutaris Hostia,

Quae coeli pandis ostium;

Bella premunt hostilia,

Da robur, fer auxilium.

Uni Trinoque Domino

Sit sempiterna gloria:

Qui vitam sine termino

Nobis donet in patria.

Amen

St Thomas Aquinas

*Let everything that lives and that breathes
give praise to the Lord.* (Ps 150:5)

O SAVING VICTIM

O Saving Victim, opening wide

The gate of Heaven to man below.

Our foes press on from every side;

Thy strength supply, Thine aid bestow.

All praise and thanks to Thee ascend,

For evermore, Bless'd Three in One.

O grant us life that shall not end

In our true native land with Thee.

Amen.

Translated by Edward Caswall

THE DIVINE PRAISES

Blessed be God.

Blessed be His holy Name.

Blessed be Jesus Christ, true God and true Man.

Blessed be the Name of Jesus.

Blessed be His most Sacred Heart.

Blessed be His most Precious Blood.

Blessed be Jesus in the most holy Sacrament of the altar.

Blessed be the Holy Spirit, the Paraclete.

Blessed be the great Mother of God, Mary most holy.

Blessed be her holy and Immaculate Conception.

Blessed be her glorious Assumption.

Blessed be the name of Mary, Virgin and Mother.

Blessed be Saint Joseph, her most chaste spouse.

Blessed be God in His Angels and in His Saints.

Worship the Lord in His temple. (Ps 95:9)

SWEET SACRAMENT DIVINE

Sweet Sacrament divine,
Hid in Thy earthly home,
Lo! round Thy lowly shrine,
With suppliant hearts we come.
Jesus, to Thee our voice we raise,
In songs of love and heartfelt praise,
Sweet Sacrament divine.

Sweet Sacrament of peace,
Dear home of every heart,
Where restless yearnings cease,
And sorrows all depart.
There in Thine ear, all trustfully
We tell our tale of misery,
Sweet Sacrament of peace.

Sweet Sacrament of rest,
Ark from the ocean's roar,
Within Thy shelter blest
Soon may we reach the shore.
Save us, for still the tempest raves;
Save, lest we sink beneath the waves,
Sweet Sacrament of rest.

Sweet Sacrament divine,
Earth's light and jubilee,
In Thy far depths doth shine
Thy Godhead's majesty.
Sweet light, so shine on us, we pray,
That earthly joys may fade away,
Sweet Sacrament divine.

Francis Stanfield

ADOREMUS

Adoremus in aeternum, Sanctissimum Sacramentum.

Laudate Dominum, omnes gentes, laudate eum,
omnes populi.
Quoniam confirmata est super nos misericordia ejus,
et veritas Domini manet in aeternum.

Gloria Patri, et Filio, et Spiritui Sancto.
Sicut erat in principio, et nunc, et semper,
et in saecula saeculorum.

Adoremus in aeternum Sanctissimum Sacramentum.

Traditional Plainsong

Before You all the earth shall bow. (Ps 65:4)

LET US ADORE

Let us adore forever the most Holy Sacrament.

Praise the Lord, all ye nations: praise Him,
all ye people.
Because His mercy is confirmed upon us;
And the truth of the Lord remaineth for ever.

Glory be to the Father, and to the Son,
and to the Holy Ghost.
As it was in the beginning, is now,
and ever shall be, world without end.

Amen.

Let us adore forever the most Holy Sacrament.

Translation Anon

PANGE LINGUA

Pange lingua gloriosi,
Corporis mysterium,
Sanguinisque pretiosi,
Quem in mundi pretium,
Fructus ventris generosi,
Rex effudit gentium.

Nobis datus, nobis natus,
Ex intacta Virgine,
Et in mundo conversatus,
Sparso verbi semine,
Sui moras incolatus,
Miro clausit ordine.

In supremae nocte coenae,
Recumbens cum fratribus,
Observata lege plene,
Cibis in legalibus,
Cibum turbae duodenae,
Se dat suis manibus.

Verbum caro panem verum
Verbo carnem efficit;
Fitque sanguis Christi merum,
Et si sensus deficit;
Ad firmandum cor sincerum
Sola fides sufficit.

St Thomas Aquinas

With songs let us hail the Lord. (Ps 94:2)

SING, MY TONGUE, THE SAVIOUR'S GLORY

Sing, my tongue, the Saviour's glory,
of His flesh the mystery sing:
of the Blood all price exceeding
shed by our immortal King,
destined for the world's redemption
from a noble womb to spring.

Of a pure and spotless virgin
born for us on earth below,
He, as man with man conversing,
stayed, the seeds of truth to sow;
then He closed in solemn order
wondrously His life of woe.

On the night of that last supper,
seated with His chosen band,
He the Paschal victim eating,
first fulfils the law's command;
then, as food to His apostles,
gives Himself with His own hand.

Word made flesh, the bread of nature
by His word to Flesh He turns;
wine into His Blood He changes:
what though sense no change discerns?
Only be the heart in earnest,
faith her lesson quickly learns.

Translation Anon

TANTUM ERGO

Tantum ergo Sacramentum

Veneremur cernui;

Et antiquum documentum,

Novo cedat ritui;

Praestet fides supplementum,

Sensuum defectui.

Genitori, Genitoque

Laus et jubilatio,

Salus, honor, virtus quoque

Sit et benedictio:

Procedenti ab utroque,

Compar sit laudatio.

St Thomas Aquinas

My heart is ready, O God;
I will sing, sing Your praise. (Ps 107:1)

TANTUM ERGO

Down in adoration falling

This Great Sacrament we hail.

Ancient types have long departed,

Newer rites of grace prevail,

Faith for all defects supplying

Where the feeble senses fail.

Glory let us give and blessing

To the Father and the Son.

Honour, might and praise addressing

While eternal ages run.

Equal praise to Him confessing

Who proceeds from both as One.

Translated by Edward Caswall

ADORO TE DEVOTE

Adoro te devote, latens Deitas,
Quæ sub his figuris vere latitas;
Tibi se cor meum totum subjicit,
Quia te contemplans totum deficit.

Visus, tactus, gustus in te fallitur,
Sed auditu solo tuto creditur.
Credo quidquid dixit Dei Filius;
Nil hoc verbo veritátis verius.

In cruce latebat sola Deitas,
At hic latet simul et Humanitas,
Ambo tamen credens atque confitens,
Peto quod petivit latro pœnitens.

Plagas, sicut Thomas, non intueor:
Deum tamen meum te confiteor.
Fac me tibi semper magis credere,
In te spem habere, te diligere.

O memoriale mortis Domini!
Panis vivus, vitam præstans homini!
Præsta meæ menti de te vívere,
Et te illi semper dulce sapere.

Pie Pelicane, Jesu Domine,
Me immundum munda tuo sanguine:
Cujus una stilla salvum facere
Totum mundum quit ab omni scelere.

Jesu, quem velatum nunc aspicio,
Oro, fiat illud quod tam sitio:
Ut te revelata cernens facie,
Visu sim beátus tuæ gloriæ.

St Thomas Aquinas

My Lover belongs to me and I to Him. (Sg 2:16)

GODHEAD HERE IN HIDING

Godhead here in hiding,
Whom I do adore
Masked by these bare shadows,
Shape and nothing more,
See, Lord, at Thy service low lies here a heart
Lost, all lost in wonder at the God Thou art.

Seeing, touching, tasting are in Thee deceived;
How says trusty hearing? That shall be believed;
What God's Son hath told me, take for truth I do;
Truth Himself speaks truly, or there's nothing true.

On the Cross Thy Godhead made no sign to men;
Here Thy very manhood steals from human ken;
Both are my confession, both are my belief,
And I pray the prayer of the dying thief.

I am not like Thomas, wounds I cannot see,
But can plainly call Thee Lord and God as he;
This faith each day deeper be my holding of,
Daily make me harder hope and dearer love.

O Thou our reminder of Christ crucified,
Living Bread, the life of us for whom He died,
Lend this life to me then; feed and feast my mind,
There be Thou the sweetness man was meant to find.

Jesu, Whom I look at shrouded here below,
I beseech Thee send me what I long for so,
Some day to gaze on Thee face to face in light
And be blest for ever with Thy glory's sight.

**Translated by
Gerard Manley Hopkins SJ**

O ESCA VIATORUM

O esca viatorum,

O panis angelorum,

O manna coelitum.

Esurientes ciba,

Dulcedine non priva,

Corda quaerentium,

Corda quaerentium.

O Jesu tuum vultum,

Quem colimus occultum

Sub panis specie.

Facut, remoto velo,

Post libera in coelo,

Cernamus facie,

Cernamus facie.

Anon
Seventeenth Century Hymn

I will sing to the Lord, the Most High. (Ps 58:18)

O ESCA VIATORUM

O Food of travellers, angels' Bread,

Manna wherewith the blest are fed,

Come nigh, and with Thy sweetness fill

The hungry hearts that seek Thee still.

O fount of love, O well unpriced,

Outpouring from the heart of Christ,

Give us to drink of very Thee,

And all we pray shall answered be.

And bring us to that time and place

When this Thy dear and veiled face

Blissful and glorious shall be seen -

Ah Jesus! with no veil between.

Translated by W.H. Shewring

TE DEUM LAUDAMUS

We praise Thee, as God.
We acknowledge Thee to be the Lord.
All the earth doth worship Thee, the Father everlasting.

To Thee all angels cry aloud,
The heavens and all the Powers therein.
To Thee Cherubim and Seraphim continually do cry:
Holy, holy, holy, Lord God of Hosts.
Heaven and earth are full of the majesty of Thy glory.

The glorious choir of the Apostles praise Thee.
The admirable company of the Prophets praise Thee.
The white-robed army of Martyrs praise Thee.
The Holy Church throughout all the world
doth acknowledge Thee.

The Father of an infinite Majesty,
Thy adorable, true and only Son.
Also the Holy Ghost, the Comforter,
Thou art the King of Glory, O Christ.

Thou art the everlasting Son of the Father.
When Thou tookest upon Thee to deliver man,
Thou didst not abhor the Virgin's womb.

When Thou hadst overcome the sting of death,
Thou didst open the kingdom of heaven to all believers.
Thou sittest at the right hand of God in the glory of the Father.

We believe that Thou shalt come to be our Judge.
We pray Thee, therefore, help Thy servants.
Whom Thou hast redeemed with Thy precious Blood.

Make them to be numbered with Thy Saints,
In glory everlasting.

O Lord, save Thy people
And bless Thine inheritance.
Govern them and lift them up for ever.

Day by day we magnify Thee
And we praise Thy name for ever,
Yea, for ever and ever.

Grant, O Lord, this day
To keep us without sin
O Lord, have mercy upon us.
Have mercy upon us.

O Lord, let Thy mercy be always upon us
As we have hoped in Thee.
O Lord, in Thee have I hoped.
Let me not be confounded for ever.

HYMN

O Jesus Christ, remember,
When Thou shalt come again,
Upon the clouds of heaven,
With all Thy shining train;
When every eye shall see Thee
In deity reveal'd,
Who now upon this altar
In silence art concealed;

Remember then, O Saviour,
I supplicate of Thee,
That here I bow'd before Thee
Upon my bended knee;
That here I owned Thy presence
And did not Thee deny,
And glorified Thy greatness
Though hid from human eye.

Accept, divine Redeemer,
The homage of my praise;
Be Thou the light and honour
And glory of my days.
Be Thou my consolation
When death is drawing nigh;
Be Thou my only treasure
Through all eternity.

Edward Caswall

3

Holy Mass

*Do this in
memory of Me*

(Lk 22:19)

He bowed His head and yielded up His spirit
(Jn. 19, 30)

This is My Body which is given up for you. (Lk 22:19)

THE MASS - HOLY SACRIFICE, SACRED BANQUET

I have earnestly desired to eat this passover with you before I suffer.

(Lk 22:15)

I will go to the altar of God,
To God, the joy of my youth.

Opening Prayer
Ordinary of the Mass
Roman Missal

O Holy Banquet!
in which Christ is received,
the memory of His Passion is renewed,
the soul is filled with grace
and a pledge of future glory is given to us,
Alleluia.

St Thomas Aquinas

O God the Father, who in Thy great and ineffable love to man didst send Thy Son into the world, to bring back the wandering sheep, turn not away Thy Face from us when we approach this Thy tremendous and unbloody Sacrifice; for we trust not to our righteousness, but to Thy gracious compassion, whereby Thou dost redeem our race.

Liturgy of St James
Ancient Devotions for Holy Communion

MEMORIAL OF HIS DEATH AND RESURRECTION

He feeds you with finest wheat. (Ps 147:14)

PREFACE FOR THE LORD'S SUPPER ON HOLY THURSDAY

Father, all-powerful and ever-living God,
we do well always and everywhere to give you thanks
through Jesus Christ our Lord.

He is the true and eternal priest
who established this unending sacrifice.
He offered himself as a victim for our deliverance
and taught us to make this offering in his memory.
As we eat his body which he gave for us,
we grow in strength.
As we drink his blood which he poured out for us,
we are washed clean.

Now, with angels and archangels,
and the whole company of heaven,
we sing the unending hymn of your praise:

Holy, holy, holy Lord, God of power and might,
heaven and earth are full of your glory.
Hosanna in the highest.
Blessed is he who comes in the name of the Lord.
Hosanna in the highest.

The Roman Missal

EVERY EUCHARISTIC CELEBRATION IS STRONGER THAN ALL THE EVIL IN THE UNIVERSE

The Eucharistic Sacrifice

It is true that the sacrifice of Calvary was enough to obtain all the graces of salvation for mankind: the Eucharistic Sacrifice but gathers the fruits. But Christ willed that His oblation should become continually present to join the Christian community together. The Eucharist is at one and the same time *Christ's Sacrifice and the Church's Sacrifice*, because in it Christ unites the Church with His redemptive work and lets the Church share in His oblation.

Personal Offering

How important it is, then, for the faithful, as they take part in the Eucharist, to assume a personal attitude of offering. It is not sufficient that they listen to the word of God, nor that they pray in common. It is necessary for them to make Christ's oblation their own, offering up their pains, their difficulties, their trials, and, even more, themselves, together with Him and in Him so as to make this gift rise even to the Father, with the gift which Christ makes of Himself.

The Mass - Triumph of Love

By entering into the Saviour's sacrificial offering, they share in the victory won by Him over the evil of the world. When we are shaken by the sight of evil spreading in the universe, with all the devastation which it produces, we should not forget that such unleashing of the forces of sin is overcome by the saving power of Christ.

Whenever the words of consecration are uttered in the Mass and the Body and Blood of Christ become present in the act of Sacrifice, the triumph of love over hatred, of holiness over sin, is also present.

Every Eucharistic celebration is stronger than all the evil in the universe; it means real, concrete accomplishment of the Redemption, and ever deeper reconciliation of sinful man with God, in prospect of a better world.

Pope John Paul II
General Audience, Rome, June 1983

PRAYER TO JESUS CHRIST

Lord Jesus Christ, Son of the living God, by the will of the Father and the work of the Holy Spirit your death brought life to the world. By your holy body and blood free me from all my sins, and from every evil. Keep me faithful to your teaching, and never let me be parted from you.

The Roman Missal
Communion Rite
Private Preparation of the Priest

May the sacred feast of Thy Table, O Lord, always strengthen and renew us, guide and protect our weakness amid the storms of the world, and bring us into the haven of everlasting salvation; through Jesus Christ our Lord.

Amen.

Leonine Sacramentary
Ancient Devotions for Holy Communion

THE MASS - THE GREATEST ACTION ON EARTH

To me nothing is so consoling, so piercing, so thrilling, so overcoming as the Mass. It is the greatest action that can be on earth. Christ is present before Whom angels bow and devils tremble.

At Mass, frail, ignorant, sinful men, by the sacerdotal power given to the priest, compel the presence of the Most High.

In Holy Communion we quench our tepidity with that love which would inflame us.

Christ in the Blessed Sacrament has made Himself weak as an example to us who are proud.

Christ is in bonds in the Blessed Sacrament. He has made Himself a prisoner so that you can come to Him.

In the Church, in the Eucharist, the Divinity has made a union between God above and man below.

Loss and Gain
John Henry Cardinal Newman

May Thy Table, O God, set us free from earthly delights, and ever supply us with celestial Food; through Jesus Christ our Lord,

Amen.

Leonine Sacramentary
Ancient Devotions for Holy Communion

You have prepared a banquet for me. (Ps 22:5)

PREFACE FOR CORPUS CHRISTI

Father, all-powerful and ever-living God,
we do well always and everywhere to give you thanks
through Jesus Christ our Lord.

At the Last Supper,
as he sat at table with his apostles,
he offered himself to you as the spotless lamb,
the acceptable gift that gives you perfect praise.
Christ has given us this memorial of his passion
to bring us its saving power until the end of time.

In this great sacrament you feed your people
and strengthen them in holiness,
so that the family of mankind
may come to walk in the light of one faith,
in one communion of love.
We come then to this wonderful Sacrament
to be fed at your table
and grow into the likeness of the risen Christ.

Earth unites with heaven
to sing the new song of creation
as we adore and praise you for ever:

Holy, holy, holy Lord, God of power and might,
heaven and earth are full of your glory.
Hosanna in the highest,
Blessed is he who comes in the name of the Lord.
Hosanna in the highest.

The Roman Missal

THE EUCHARIST: SOURCE OF CHRISTIAN SPIRIT

It is from the Eucharist that all of us receive the grace and strength for daily living - to live real Christian lives, in the joy of knowing that God loves us, that Christ died for us, and that the Holy Spirit lives in us.

Our full participation in the Eucharist is the real source of the Christian spirit that we wish to see in our personal lives and in all aspects of society. Whether we serve in politics, in the economic, cultural, social or scientific field - no matter what our occupation is - the Eucharist is a challenge to our daily lives.

Dear brothers and sisters: there must always be consistency between what we believe and what we do. We cannot live on the glories of our past Christian history. Our union with Christ in the Eucharist must be expressed in the truth of our lives today - in our actions, in our behaviour, in our life-style, and in our relationships with others.

For each one of us the Eucharist is a call to ever greater effort, so that we may live as true followers of Jesus: truthful in our speech, generous in our deeds, concerned, respectful of the dignity and rights of all persons, whatever their rank or income, self-sacrificing, fair and just, kind, considerate, compassionate and self-controlled - looking to the well-being of our families, our young people, our country, Europe and the world.

The truth of our union with Jesus Christ in the Eucharist is tested by whether or not we really love our fellow men and women; it is tested by how we treat others; especially our families, husbands and wives, children and parents, brothers and sisters. It is tested by whether or not we try to be reconciled with our enemies, on whether or not we forgive those who hurt us or offend us. It is tested by whether we practise in life what our faith teaches us. We must always remember what Jesus said: *"You are My friends if you do what I command you"*. (Jn 14:14).

Pope John Paul II
General Audience, 1979

We beseech Thee, O Lord, mercifully to grant to Thy Church the gifts of unity and peace, which are mystically figured under the gifts we offer. Through Thy Son, Jesus Christ our Lord, who liveth and reigneth with Thee, in the unity of the Holy Spirit, God, for ever and ever.

Amen.

Secret
Votive Mass of Blessed Sacrament
Latin Rite
Ancient Devotions for Holy Communion

THE SACRIFICE OF CALVARY

We believe that the Mass, celebrated by the priest representing the person of Christ by virtue of the power received through the Sacrament of Orders, and offered by him in the name of Christ and the members of His Mystical Body, is the Sacrifice of Calvary rendered sacramentally present on our altars.

We believe that as the bread and wine consecrated by the Lord at the Last Supper were changed into His body and His blood which were to be offered for us on the cross, likewise the bread and wine consecrated by the priest are changed into the body and blood of Christ enthroned gloriously in heaven, and we believe that the mysterious presence of the Lord, under what continues to appear to our senses as before, is a true, real and substantial presence.

Transubstantiation

Christ cannot be thus present in this sacrament except by the change into His body of the reality itself of the bread and the change into His blood of the reality itself of the wine, leaving unchanged only the properties of the bread and wine which our senses perceive. This mysterious change is very appropriately called by the Church *transubstantiation*.

Every theological explanation which seeks some understanding of this mystery must, in order to be in accord with Catholic faith, maintain that in the reality itself, independently of our mind, the bread and wine have ceased to exist after the Consecration, so that it is the adorable body and blood of the Lord Jesus that from then on are really before us under the sacramental species of bread and wine, as the Lord willed it, in order to give Himself to us as food and to associate us with the unity of His Mystical Body.

The unique and indivisible existence of the Lord glorious in heaven is not multiplied, but is rendered present by the sacrament in the many places on earth where Mass is celebrated. And this existence remains present, after the sacrifice, in the Blessed Sacrament which is, in the tabernacle, the living heart of each of our churches. And it is our very sweet duty to honour and adore in the blessed Host which our eyes see, the Incarnate Word Whom they cannot see, and Who, without leaving heaven, is made present before us.

Pope Paul VI
The Credo of the People of God, **1968**

O God,
Who in this wonderful Sacrament
have left us a memorial of Thy Passion,
grant us, we beseech Thee,
so to venerate the sacred mysteries of Thy Body and Blood
that we may ever perceive within us the fruit of Thy redemption.

Collect for Corpus Christi
Roman Missal

O God the Bread of our life, look upon us; be Thou the Guardian of our bodies; be Thou the Saviour of our souls.

Gallican Missal
Ancient Devotions for Holy Communion

Do this in remembrance of Me. (1 Cor 11:25)

WE ARE ONE BODY

For I received from the Lord what I also delivered to you, that the Lord Jesus on the night when He was betrayed took bread, and when He had given thanks, He broke it, and said,

> *This is My Body which is for you.*
> *Do this in remembrance of Me.*

In the same way also the cup, after supper, saying,

> *This cup is the new covenant in My Blood.*
> *Do this, as often as you drink it,*
> *in remembrance of Me.*

(1 Cor 11:23-25)

The cup of blessing which we bless, is it not a participation in the Blood of Christ? The Bread which we break, is it not a participation in the Body of Christ? Because there is one Bread, we who are many are one body, for we all partake of the one Bread.

(1 Cor 10:16-17)

THE EUCHARIST COMMITS US TO THE POOR

To receive in truth the Body and Blood of Christ given up for us, we must recognise Christ in the poorest, His brethren:

> You have tasted the Blood of the Lord, yet you do not recognise your brother ... You dishonour this table when you do not judge worthy of sharing your food someone judged worthy to take part in this meal ... God freed you from all your sins and invited you here, but you have not become more merciful.[1]

Catechism of the Catholic Church
Para 1397

1. St John Chrysostom

THE EUCHARIST AND THE UNITY OF CHRISTIANS

Before the greatness of this mystery St Augustine exclaims, *"O Sacrament of devotion! O sign of unity! O bond of charity!"* The more painful the experience of the divisions in the Church which break the common participation in the table of the Lord, the more urgent are our prayers to the Lord that the time of complete unity among all who believe in Him may return.

Ibid, Para 1398

He satisfies the thirsty souls
He fills the hungry with good things. (Ps 106:9)

JESUS IN OUR MIDST

If we really understand the Eucharist,

If we really centre our lives on Jesus' Body and Blood,

If we nourish our lives with the Bread of the Eucharist,

It will be easy for us to see Christ in that hungry one next door,

the one lying in the gutter,

that alcoholic man we shun,

our husband or our wife, or our restless child.

For in them, we will recognise the distressing disguises of the poor: Jesus in our midst.

Mother Teresa
Loving Jesus

May the Communion of Thy Sacrament, O Lord, both purify us and make us one, through Jesus Christ our Lord.

Amen.

Gelasian Sacramentary
Ancient Devotions for Holy Communion

THE EUCHARIST - SECRET OF LOVE

Together with Christ, we celebrate in the Eucharist His loving dedication to the Father and in intimate union with Him through our receiving His Body and Blood in Sacrifice, we become ourselves an altar in the Holy Spirit and a gift that is pleasing to God. In this way the Eucharist is at once the summit of the spiritual life of the Christian and the source of his spirituality.

That is why St Gregory the Great asked: *"What is the altar of God if not the heart of those who lead a good (Christian) life?"*

The secret of the Eucharist is a *secret of love* which imposes on us its own obligation. Union in the breaking of the Eucharistic Bread makes us even more sensitive to the misfortune, the hunger and the suffering of our fellow man.

When we eat the Bread, with which Christ gives us life from His divine life, then we too must be ready to share our life with our neighbour. If we find nourishment for ourselves from this source of love, then we too are called not simply to give something, but to offer our very selves in the service of our neighbour. The early Christian community illustrated this in an exemplary way.

That was why the pagans could say in admiration of those Christians: *"See how they love one another"*.

Pope John Paul II
Switzerland, June 1984

*I am the living Bread
which came down from heaven.* (Jn 6:51)

THE REIGN OF THE EUCHARIST

The reign of the Eucharist is the reign of the Church. Where the Eucharist is neglected, the Church has none but unfaithful children, and she will soon have to deplore fresh ruins.

St Peter Julian Eymard
The Real Presence - Eucharistic Meditations

In the tumultuous events of our time, it is important to look to the Eucharist: it must be at the heart of the life of priests and consecrated people; the light and strength of spouses in putting into practice their commitment to fidelity, chastity and the apostolate; the ideal in education and in training children, adolescents and young people; the comfort and support of those who are troubled, of the sick and all who are weeping in the Gethsemane of life.

It must be for everyone the incentive to fulfil the testament of divine charity in humble and joyous availability to our brothers and sisters, as the Lord taught by His own example, washing the Apostles' feet.

Pope John Paul II
General Audience, Rome, April 1995

JESUS REMAINS WITH US

Christ remains in our midst not only during the Mass, but also afterwards, under the species reserved in the tabernacle. The Eucharistic worship extends throughout the whole day, without being limited to the celebration of the Sacrifice. He is a God Who is near, a God Who waits for us, a God Who has chosen to remain with us.

When one has faith in this Real Presence, how easy it is to be close to Him, adoring the Love of loves, how easy it is to understand the expressions of love with which, throughout the centuries, Christians have surrounded the Eucharist.

Not only do we receive Christ, but Christ too receives each of us. In this Sacrament He accepts man always, so to speak; He makes him His friend, as He said in the Upper Room: "You are My friends" (Jn 15:14). This welcome and acceptance of man by Christ is an extraordinary favour. Man feels very deeply the desire to be accepted. All man's life turns in this direction, that he may be welcomed and accepted by God; and the Eucharist expresses that sacramentally.

Yet man must, as St Paul says, "examine himself" (cf. 1 Cor 11: 28), to see if he is worthy of being accepted by Christ. The Eucharist is, in a certain sense, a constant challenge to man to try to be accepted, to adapt his conscience to the demands of holy divine Friendship.

Pope John Paul II
Eucharistic Congress, Peru, 1988

You give them their fill of Your treasures. (Ps 16:14)

HOW PRECIOUS AND ADMIRABLE IS THIS BANQUET!

O banquet most precious! O banquet most admirable! O banquet overflowing with every spiritual delicacy! Can anything be more excellent than the repast, in which not the flesh of goats and heifers as of old, but Christ the true God, is given us for nourishment?

What more wondrous than this holy sacrament! In it bread and wine are changed substantially, and under the appearance of a little bread and wine is had Christ Jesus, God and perfect Man. In this sacrament sins are purged away, virtues are increased, the soul is satiated with an abundance of every spiritual gift; no other sacrament is so beneficial. Since it was instituted unto the salvation of all, it is offered by Holy Church for the living and for the dead, that all may share in its treasures.

My dearly beloved, is it not beyond human power to express the ineffable delicacy of this sacrament in which spiritual sweetness is tasted in its very source, in which is brought to mind the remembrance of that all-excelling charity which Christ showed in His sacred Passion?

Surely it was to impress more profoundly upon the hearts of the faithful the immensity of this charity that our loving Saviour instituted this sacrament at the last supper when, having celebrated the Pasch with His disciples, He was about to leave the world and return to the Father. It was to serve as an unending remembrance of His Passion, as the fulfilment of ancient types - this the greatest of His miracles. To those who sorrow over His departure He has given a unique solace.

St Thomas Aquinas
Lessons for Corpus Christi

Hic est enim calix sanguinis mei.

Eternal Father, I offer You the Body and Blood, Soul and Divinity of Your dearly beloved Son, our Lord Jesus Christ, in atonement for our sins and those of the whole world.

Prayer given to St Maria Faustina Kowalska
Divine Mercy in my Soul

My mouth shall declare Your praise. (Ps 50:17)

OUR GOD IS SO NEAR TO US

The immeasurable kindness of the divine generosity, which is offered to Christians in the sacraments, bestows on them an inestimable dignity. There was never a people so distinguished that had the Divinity so near to it as our God is to us.

The only-begotten Son of God, Who wished to share His divinity with us, assumed our human nature to make us divine. Still more He left as a lasting reminder of this great deed His Body as food and His Blood as drink under the species of bread and wine.

St Thomas Aquinas
Lessons for Corpus Christi

I dare to say that God, though He be omnipotent,
could not give us more;
though He be all wise, knows not how to give us more;
though He be all rich, has not more to give.

St Augustine of Hippo

O Taste and see that the Lord is good: He that is broken, and not divided, distributed to the faithful, and not consumed, for the remission of their sins and eternal life, now and ever, and to all ages.

Liturgy of St James
Ancient Devotions for Holy Communion

HYMN OF PRAISE

The immolated Christ is distributed amongst us.
    Alleluia!

He gives us His Body as food
And His Blood He pours out over us.
    Alleluia!

Draw near to the Lord and be filled with His light.
    Alleluia!

Taste and see how sweet is the Lord.
    Alleluia!

Bless the Lord in the Heavens.
    Alleluia!

Bless Him in the highest Heavens.
    Alleluia!

Bless Him, all ye His angels.
    Alleluia!

Bless Him, all ye powers.
    Alleluia!

Armenian Liturgy

4

Preparation for Holy Communion

*Lord,
I am not worthy*

(Mt 8:8)

THE BREAD OF LIFE

I am the Bread of life; he who comes to Me shall not hunger, and he who believes in Me shall never thirst.

(Jn 6:35)

I place myself in Your presence. I adore You, my Saviour. I praise You and I offer myself wholly to You, the true Bread of my soul, and my everlasting joy.

John Henry Cardinal Newman

I am the Bread of life. (Jn 6:35)

PRAYER BEFORE HOLY COMMUNION

Almighty, Everlasting God, lo, I draw near to the Sacrament of Thine Only-begotten Son, our Lord Jesus Christ. As sick, I approach to the Physician of Life; unclean, to the Fountain of Mercy; blind, to the Light of eternal Brightness; poor and needy, to the Lord of heaven and earth.

I implore Thee, therefore, out of the abundance of Thy boundless mercy, that Thou wouldst deign to heal my sickness, to wash my defilements, to enlighten my blindness, to enrich my poverty, and to clothe my nakedness; that I may receive the Bread of Angels, the King of kings, the Lord of lords, with such reverence and humility, such contrition and devotion, such purity and faith, such purpose and intention, as is expedient for the health of my soul.

Grant, I beseech Thee, that I may receive not only the Sacrament of the Body and Blood of the Lord, but also the whole grace and virtue of that Sacrament.

O most merciful God, grant me so to receive the Body of Thine Only-begotten Son, our Lord Jesus Christ, which He took of the Virgin Mary, that I may be found worthy to be incorporated into His mystical Body, and accounted among His members. And, O most loving Father, grant that He Whom now I purpose to receive under a veil I may at last behold with unveiled face, even Thy beloved Son, Who with Thee and the Holy Ghost ever liveth and reigneth, one God, world without end.

Amen.

St Thomas Aquinas

THE EUCHARIST TRANSFORMS US INTO JESUS

God became a man in order to save us. When He had become a man, however, He desired to become food so that, feeding ourselves on Him, each of us might become another Jesus. Now, it is one thing to see Jesus as if we had lived in His times; it is another thing to re-live Jesus, to be able to be another Jesus upon earth today. The Eucharist has precisely this purpose: to nourish us with Jesus in order to transform us into another Jesus because He has loved us as Himself.

The flesh on which we are nourished is a glorified flesh, the same flesh that Jesus possesses where He sits at the right hand of the Father. From this glorified flesh, which gives divine life, there is an outflowing of the Holy Spirit, who forms Christ in us because we have been fed with the Eucharist.

Chiara Lubich
The Eucharist

THE EUCHARIST CHANGES OUR LIVES

Proclaiming the death of the Lord *"until he comes"* (1 Cor 11.26) entails that all who take part in the Eucharist be committed to changing their lives and making them in a certain way completely "Eucharistic". It is this fruit of a transfigured existence and a commitment to transforming the world in accordance with the Gospel which splendidly illustrates the eschatological tension inherent in the celebration of the Eucharist and in the Christian life as a whole: *"Come, Lord Jesus!"* (Rev 22:20)

Pope John Paul II
Ecclesia de Eucharistia, **2003**

If any man thirst, let him come to Me. (Jn 7:37)

SEVENTH CENTURY HYMN

At the Lamb's high feast we sing
Praise to our victorious King,
Who hath washed us in the tide
Flowing from His pierced side.
Praise we Him Whose love divine
Gives the guests His Blood for wine,
Gives His Body for the feast,
Love the victim, love the priest.

Where the Paschal Blood is poured,
Death's dark angel sheathes his sword;
Israel's host triumphant go
Through the wave that drowns the foe.
Christ, the Lamb, Whose Blood was shed,
Paschal victim, Paschal Bread;
With sincerity and love
Eat we manna from above.

Mighty victim from the sky,
Powers of hell beneath Thee lie;
Death is conquered in the fight;
Thou has brought us life and light.
Now Thy banner Thou dost wave;
Vanquished Satan and the grave;
Angels join His praise to tell -
See o'erthrown the prince of hell.

Paschal triumph, Paschal joy,
Only sin can this destroy;
From the death of sin set free,
Souls re-born, dear Lord, in Thee.
Hymns of glory, songs of praise,
Father, unto Thee we raise;
Risen Lord, all praise to Thee,
Ever with the Spirit be.

Translated by R. Campbell

THE KING'S FEAST

What indeed is required of us in order that we may sit down at the great King's Feast and eat with profit the heavenly Bread? That we come to it clad in the "wedding garment," that is to say that we should be in a state of grace, and have a right intention.

Nothing more is required on our side. But for Jesus? Certainly it was not without labour that He prepared this feast for us. It needed the self abasements of the Incarnation, the humility and obscure labours of the hidden life, the fatigue of the apostolate, the conflicts with the Pharisees, the combats against the prince of darkness, finally, that which contains and crowns all, the sufferings of the Passion. It was only at the cost of His bloodstained immolation and untold sufferings that Christ Jesus merited for us this wonderful grace of being united so closely to Himself in that He nourishes us with His Sacred Body, and gives us His Precious Blood to drink.

Therefore it was that He instituted this Sacrament on the eve of His Passion as if to give us the most touching proof of the excess of His love for us. It is because it is communicated to us at such a price that this gift is full of the sweetness of the infinite love of Jesus Christ.

These are some of the marvels figured by the manna and brought about, for the life and joy of our souls, by the wisdom and bounty of our God.

How is it possible not to "admire" these marvels of the Church? How can we fail to surround these sacred mysteries with all our reverence and adoration?

Blessed Columba Marmion, Abbot
Christ in His Mysteries

Behold, the Lamb of God! (Jn 1:36)

THE LAMB DESTROYS THE POWER OF THE DEVIL

Good Lord, which upon the sacrifice of the paschal lamb didst so clearly destroy the first-begotten children of the Egyptians, that Pharao was thereby forced to let the children of Israel depart out of his bondage, I beseech Thee give me the grace in such faithful wise to receive the very sweet Paschal Lamb, the very blessed Body of our sweet Saviour Thy Son, that, the first suggestions of sin by Thy power killed in my heart, I may safe depart out of the danger of the most cruel Pharao the devil.

St Thomas More
Treatise on the Passion
Tower of London, 1534

We beseech Thee, O Lord, that the solemn reception of Thy Sacrament may cleanse us from all our old sins, and change us into new creatures; through Jesus Christ our Lord.

Leonine Sacramentary
Ancient Devotions for Holy Communion

HOLY COMMUNION, FEAST OF THE SOUL

Nothing is so joyous as a feast; Holy Communion is the feast of the soul, that is to say, a source of deepest joys. Why should not Christ Jesus, Truth and Life, principle of all being and of all beatitude, fill our hearts with joy? Why, in making us drink from the chalice of His Divine Blood, should He not pour into our souls that spiritual gladness which excites charity and sustains fervour? See Him in the supper room, after He has instituted this Divine Sacrament. He speaks to His Apostles of His joy; He desires that this joy, His own joy, altogether divine, should become ours, and that our hearts should be filled with it: *Ut gaudium meum in vobis sit.*[1] It is one of the effects of the Eucharist when received with devotion - to fill the soul with supernatural sweetness that renders it prompt and devoted in God's service.

Let us not forget, however, that this joy is above all spiritual. The Eucharist being eminently the "mystery of faith," it may happen that God permits that this altogether inward joy should not react upon the sensible part of our being. It may happen that very fervent souls remain in a state of great dryness and aridity after having received the Bread of life. Do not let them be astonished at this: above all never let them be discouraged; if they have brought all the good dispositions possible for receiving Christ, and still suffer from their powerlessness, let them be reassured and remain in peace. Christ, ever living, acts in silence, but sovereignly in the innermost depths of the soul in order to transform it into Himself; that is the most precious effect of this heavenly food: *"He that eateth My Flesh, and drinketh My Blood, abideth in Me, and I in him".*[2]

Blessed Columba Marmion, Abbot
Christ in His Mysteries

1. *That My joy may be in you* (Jn 15:11)

2. Jn 6:56

*I have earnestly desired
to eat this passover with you.* (Lk 22:15)

HE IN US AND WE IN HIM

See, dearest daughter, in what an excellent state is the soul who receives, as she should, this Bread of Life, this Food of the Angels. By receiving this Sacrament she dwells in Me and I in her, as the fish in the sea, and the sea in the fish.

In that soul grace dwells, for, since she has received this Bread of Life in a state of grace, My grace remains in her, after the accidents of bread have been consumed. I leave you the imprint of grace, as does a seal, which, when lifted from the hot wax upon which it has been impressed, leaves behind its imprint, so the virtue of this Sacrament remains in the soul, that is to say, the heat of My Divine charity and the clemency of the Holy Spirit.

The imprint remains, when the seal has been taken away, that is, when the material accidents of the bread, having been consumed, this True Sun has returned to Its Centre, not that it was ever really separated from It, but constantly united to Me.

See then how straitly you are constrained and obliged to render Me love, because I love you so much, and, being the Supreme and Eternal Goodness, deserve your love.

St Catherine of Siena
The Dialogue of the Seraphic Virgin

PRAYER OF ST AMBROSE

O gracious Lord Jesus Christ, I a sinner, nothing presuming on my own deserts, but trusting in Thy mercy and goodness, with fear and trembling approach to the Table of Thy most sweet Feast. For my heart and body are stained with many sins, my thoughts and lips not diligently guarded.

Wherefore, O gracious God, O awful Majesty, in my extremity I turn to Thee, the Fount of Mercy; to Thee I hasten to be healed, and take refuge under Thy protection; and Thee, before Whom as my Judge I cannot stand, I long for as my Saviour.

To Thee, O Lord, I show my wounds, to Thee I lay bare my shame. I know my sins are many and great, for which I am afraid. My trust is in Thy mercies, of which there is no end.

Look therefore upon me with the eyes of Thy mercy, O Lord Jesus Christ, God and Man, crucified for man; hearken unto me, whose trust is in Thee; have mercy upon me, who am full of sin and misery, O Thou fount of mercy, that wilt never cease to flow.

Hail, saving Victim, offered for me and all mankind on the Cross of suffering and shame. Hail, noble and precious Blood, flowing from the wounds of my crucified Lord and Saviour Jesus Christ, and washing away the sins of the whole world.

Be mindful, O Lord, of Thy creature, whom Thou hast redeemed with Thine own Blood. I repent that I have sinned; I desire to amend what I have done.

Take therefore away from me, O most merciful Father, all my iniquities and sins: that, being cleansed both in body and soul, I may worthily taste the Holy of Holies; and grant that this holy feeding on Thy Body and Blood, of which, unworthy as I am, I purpose to partake, may be for the remission of my sins, and the perfect cleansing of all my offences, for the driving away of all evil thoughts and the renewal of all holy desires, for the healthful bringing forth of fruit well-pleasing unto Thee, and the most sure protection of my soul and body against the wiles of all my enemies.

Amen.

Lord our God, Heavenly Bread, Life of the world, I have sinned against heaven and before Thee, and am not worthy to partake of Thy spotless Mysteries: but do Thou, Who art a compassionate God, make me worthy by Thy grace to partake, without condemnation, of Thy holy Body and precious Blood, for the remission of sins, and eternal life.

Liturgy of St James
Ancient Devotions for Holy Communion

Hear us, O Lord Jesus Christ our God, out of Thy holy dwelling-place, and from the throne of the glory of Thy kingdom; come and sanctify us, Thou that sitteth above with the Father, and art here invisibly present with us; and by Thy mighty hand make us, and all Thy people, worthy to partake of Thy spotless Body and precious Blood.

Liturgy of St John Chrysostom
Ancient Devotions for Holy Communion

Lord I am not worthy. (Mt 8:8)

PRAYERS

Happy and blessed are you, O Joseph, to whom it was given not only to see and to hear that God Whom many kings desired to see and saw not, to hear and heard not; but also to bear Him in your arms, to embrace Him, to clothe Him and to guard and defend Him.

V Pray for us, O blessed Joseph,
R That we may be made worthy of the promises of Christ.

O God, Who has given us a royal Priesthood, grant to us we beseech You, that as Blessed Joseph was found worthy to handle with his hands, and to bear within his arms, Your Only-begotten Son, born of the Virgin Mary, so may we be made fit, by cleanness of heart and innocence of works, to wait upon Your Holy Altars that we may worthily receive the Most Sacred Body and Blood of Your Son now in this present world, and deserve to attain an everlasting reward in the world to come. Through the same Christ our Lord, Amen.

Ancient Devotions for Holy Communion

In your arms, Joseph, you carried
the Bread of Life come down from heaven
for the life of the world.
At Bethlehem, in Egypt, in Nazareth
you provided for Him a home,
the best you could.
Come to my aid and help me to prepare my heart
as best I can,
so as to receive with faith and to house with charity,
the Christ who comes to me in this great Sacrament.

Brian Moore SJ
Devotions to St Joseph

THE EUCHARIST AND PENANCE

In the Encyclical *Redemptor Hominis* I have already drawn attention to the close link between the Sacrament of Penance and the Sacrament of the Eucharist. It is not only that Penance leads to the Eucharist, but that the Eucharist also leads to Penance. For when we realise Who it is that we receive in Eucharistic Communion, there springs up in us almost spontaneously a sense of unworthiness, together with sorrow for our sins and an interior need for purification.

But we must always take care that this great meeting with Christ in the Eucharist does not become a mere habit, and that we do not receive Him unworthily, that is to say in a state of mortal sin. The practice of the virtue of penance and the Sacrament of Penance are essential for sustaining in us and continually deepening that spirit of veneration which man owes to God Himself and to His love so marvellously revealed.

Pope John Paul II
Letter on the Mystery and Worship of the Holy Eucharist, **1980**

For a constant and speedy advancement in the path of virtue we highly recommend the pious practice of frequent confession, introduced by the Church under the guidance of the Holy Ghost; for by this means we grow in a true knowledge of ourselves and in Christian humility, bad habits are uprooted, spiritual negligence and apathy are prevented, the conscience is purified and the will strengthened, salutary spiritual direction is obtained, and grace is increased by the efficacy of the sacrament itself.

Pope Pius XII
Mystici Corporis, **1943**

Have mercy on me, Lord. (Ps 6:33)

GOD ALONE MAKES US WORTHY

I beseech Thee, O God, cleanse me that I may approach Thine holy altar without stain, for I am an unworthy servant. I have sinned and transgressed before Thee and am not fitted to come nigh to Thine altar and Thy Mysteries. But mindful of Thy loving kindness and compassion, O Clemency, O Mercy, O Thou Who lovest men, I implore Thee to look with mercy upon me. Grant that I may keep myself in Thy presence, now and at all times; grant that the grace of Thine Holy Spirit may come upon me and wash away my sins.

Sanctify this offering and through it give pardon of faults and remission of sins to those for whom I would pray: to my father and my mother, and to all those living and dead who have been joined with me and have shared my sorrows, and to all the faithful. Remember them, O Lord, in Thy kingdom, and lead them among the saints and the just who have accomplished Thy will by their good works; through the intercession of our Lady, Mother of Light, of St John the Baptiser, and of all the saints.

Prayers from the Eastern Liturgies: Maronite

As often as ye shall eat this Bread, and drink the Chalice, ye shall show forth the death of the Lord, until He comes. Therefore whosoever shall eat this Bread or drink the Chalice of the Lord unworthily, shall be guilty of the Body and Blood of the Lord.

Communion
Votive Mass of the Blessed Sacrament
Latin Rite
Ancient Devotions for Holy Communion

PRAYER BEFORE HOLY COMMUNION

Most Holy Spirit,
love of the Father and the Son,
come to purify and adorn my soul,
that it may be agreeable to my Saviour
and that I may receive Him
for His glory and my salvation.

With all my heart I desire You, O Bread of Angels!
Do not look on my unworthiness
which separates me from You,
but look on Your love
which so often has invited me to
approach You.

Give Yourself wholly to me
please, O my God,
and may Your precious Body, Your holy Soul,
and Your glorious Divinity
that I adore in this most Holy Sacrament,
take entire possession of me.

O sweet Jesus! O good Jesus!
My God and my all,
have mercy
on all the souls redeemed by Your precious Blood.

Touch them forcefully
with a spark of Your love
in order to make them grateful for the love
which has made You give Yourself to us
in this most Holy Sacrament.

I offer You the glory
intrinsic to Your very being
which You have from all eternity
and all the graces that You have given
to the Blessed Virgin and to all the Saints,
with the glory that they will render You eternally
through this very love!

Prier avec Louise de Marillac
translated by Audrey English

A PRAYER WHILE AWAITING THE BLESSED SACRAMENT

At Thy feet, O my Jesus, I cast myself and I offer Thee the repentance of my contrite heart, which is humbled in its nothingness and in Thy holy presence. I adore Thee in the Sacrament of Thy love, the ineffable Eucharist.

I desire to receive Thee into the poor dwelling that my heart offers Thee. While waiting for the happiness of sacramental Communion, I wish to possess Thee in spirit.

Come to me, O my Jesus, since I, for my part, am coming to Thee! May Thy love embrace my whole being in life and in death. I believe in Thee, I hope in Thee, I love Thee.

Amen.

Raphael Cardinal Merry del Val

ABOUT OUR PREPARATION FOR HOLY COMMUNION

We have to prove ourselves, examine ourselves, purify ourselves. For it is in the highest degree right and fitting that, with great care and great devotion, we should make ourselves ready to receive food so holy and so adorable as this. In it we receive the Lord of all the earth.

Priests and people alike must come with holy fear and love to this heavenly feast. Even in the old law, God ordered the priests to sanctify themselves when they drew near to Him, lest He should strike them. Much more should we prepare ourselves when we draw near to the very city of the living God, and to God Himself Who is the Judge of all.

St Thomas Aquinas

*My soul is longing for the Lord
more than watchmen for daybreak.* (Ps 129:6)

PRAYER BEFORE COMMUNION

O Lord Jesus Christ, Whom I hope to receive in a few days within the temple of my soul, I come to implore that Thou wilt Thyself prepare Thy destined abode, cleansing it from every stain, and enriching it with an increase of faith, hope and charity, true contrition and profound humility. Grant me to sigh, with holy Simeon, for Thy coming, and, like him, to centre in Thee alone the ardent affections and fervent desires of my heart.

O Lord, Whose throne is surrounded by cherubim and seraphim, Whose presence is felt by all creation, Whose spotless sanctity the angels themselves contemplate with awe, I acknowledge my extreme unworthiness to receive Thee, but animated with lively confidence, in Thy paternal goodness, I beseech Thee to prepare me Thyself and to supply from the treasury of Thy abundant mercies for all my deficiencies.

O Thou, Who hast come on earth to save me, and Who, by Thy sufferings, hast opened heaven to receive me, grant me grace to profit from all Thou hast done and endured for my salvation.

Ancient Devotions for Holy Communion

The Body of our Lord Jesus Christ
preserve my soul unto life everlasting. *Amen.*

The Blood of our Lord Jesus Christ
preserve my soul unto life everlasting. *Amen.*

Priest's Prayer before Communion
The Roman Missal

JESUS SATISFIES ALL OUR LONGINGS

Arouse in the hearts of those under your care, Venerable Brethren, an eager and almost insatiable hunger for Jesus Christ; as a result of your teaching let the altars be thronged with children and adolescents, offering themselves, their innocence and their energetic enthusiasm to the divine Redeemer.

Let married people come in their crowds, so that from the food they receive at the sacred Table they may derive the power to train their children to be like Jesus Christ and to love Him.

Let workers be urged to receive the food that will effectively and unfailingly restore their strength and prepare an everlasting reward in heaven for their labours.

Invite them all, men and women, of every class and degree, and compel them to come in, for this is the bread of life of which they all stand in need. This is the only bread the Church of Jesus Christ has at her disposal; a bread to satisfy all the longings of our souls, to unite them closely to Jesus Christ, to form into 'one body' and one community of brethren all those who sit at the same heavenly Table, so that breaking one bread they may receive the medicine that gives immortality.

Pope Pius XII
Mediator Dei, **1947**

My soul shall be filled as with a banquet. (Ps 62:6)

PRAYER FROM AN EASTERN LITURGY

Filled with the deepest awe, let us pray before the altar of God with faith and holiness; with a pure conscience, cleansed by contrition; without hypocrisy or deceit; not with a wavering spirit, lacking in faith, but with upright actions, sincere thoughts, submissive hearts and complete trust.

Filled with charity and fruitful in good works, let us be constant in prayer before the holy altar, and we shall find grace in the day of God's manifestation and in the second coming of our Lord and Saviour Jesus Christ, Who is pitiful towards us and redeems us.

Armenian Liturgy

Receiving the Cup of the Lord's passion, and tasting the sweetness of His most holy Body, let us give thanks and praise to Him, walking in His house with joy and gladness.

Mozarabic Missal

SHORT PRAYERS BEFORE HOLY COMMUNION

Come, Lord Jesus
Come, O Lord, and do not delay
My Lord and my God!

Lord, I am not worthy to receive You.

You are the Christ, the Son of the living God!

Most Sacred Heart of Jesus, have mercy on us!

My Jesus, mercy!
O Jesus in the Blessed Sacrament, have mercy on us!
My Jesus, I love You.

My God, I believe in You, I hope in You,
I love You with all my heart.

Blessed be God.
Blessed be Jesus Christ, true God and true Man.
Blessed be Jesus in the Most Holy Sacrament of the altar.

My soul glorifies the Lord.
O God, You are my God, for You I long;
for You my soul is thirsting.
My body pines for You
like a dry weary land without water. (Ps 62).

Like the deer that yearns for running streams
so my soul is yearning for You, my God. (Ps 41).

One thing I have asked of the Lord, this will I seek after:
that I may dwell in the house of the Lord all the days of my life.

O taste and see that the Lord is sweet:
blessed is the man that hopeth in Him.

Happy are those servants whom the Lord when He cometh
shall find watching.

If any man will come after Me, let him deny himself,
and take up his cross, and follow Me.

Praise and adoration ever more
be given to the most Holy Sacrament.

O Sacrament most holy, O Sacrament divine!
All praise and all thanksgiving be every moment Thine!

I adore Thee every moment,
O living Bread from heaven,
Great Sacrament.

Jesus, my God, I adore Thee here present
in the Sacrament of Thy love!

OUR NEED FOR HIM

At the moment of receiving Communion, say to Jesus, *"Jesus, I come to You because I am weak, because I am miserable, because I am a sinner. I come to You because I have so much need of You."* What a beautiful preparation for Communion! Do not say to Him, *"I come to You because I am well prepared,"* but, *"I come to You because I need You so much."*

It is an exclusive right of the weak and miserable to be able to pray this prayer, with even greater fervour: *"I need You, and I am happy to be in such great need of Your mercy"* - a prayer which goes like an arrow straight to the depths of His infinitely merciful Heart.

Père Jean du Coeur de Jésus d'Elbée
I Believe in Love

5

Holy Communion and Thanksgiving

Give us this day our daily Bread

(Mt 6:11)

Caro mea vere est cibus et sanguis meus vere est potus.

Take, this is My Body. (Mk 14:22)

HOLY COMMUNION

O most Sacred, most loving Heart of Jesus, Thou art concealed in the Holy Eucharist, and Thou beatest for us still. Now as then Thou sayest, "Desiderio desideravi - With desire I have desired". I worship Thee then with all my best love and awe, with my fervent affection, with my most subdued, most resolved will.

O my God, when Thou dost condescend to suffer me to receive Thee, to eat and drink Thee, and Thou for a while takest up Thy abode within me, O make my heart beat with Thy Heart. Purify it of all that is earthly, all that is proud and sensual, all that is hard and cruel, of all perversity, of all disorder, of all deadness. So fill it with Thee that neither the events of the day nor the circumstances of the time may have power to ruffle it, but that in Thy love and Thy fear it may have peace.

John Henry Cardinal Newman
Meditations and Devotions

Behold, I approach the Divine Communion;
My Creator, consume me not in the partaking of it,
For Thou art a consuming fire to the unworthy;
Purify me now from every stain.

St Simeon
Ancient Devotions for Holy Communion

THE EFFECTS OF HOLY COMMUNION

What happens in Holy Communion?

Christ Our Lord and Saviour unites Himself to us in a visible way, visible in so far as He comes to us under the appearances of bread. This, surely, is a sublime condescension, which we can never sufficiently admire.

In Holy Communion Jesus works on our souls.

What He works out in us is God's highest self-communication, His incredible self-surrender to the soul. By giving us sanctifying grace, Christ unites us to the Blessed Trinity. Through His sacred Humanity we become partakers of His Divinity. Through the Son we are united to the Father and the Holy Ghost and share in the splendour of Their eternal life. He thus turns the incurable restlessness of the soul to its true object, gives it an anticipation of heaven.

In Holy Communion He intensifies our divine life, our union with the Infinite. He makes God penetrate more deeply into the essence and faculties of the soul - like fire permeating a piece of iron.

Joseph Putz SJ
My Mass

We will come to him and make Our home with him. (Jn 14:23)

PRAYER OF THANKSGIVING AND PETITION

I render thanks to Thee, O Lord, Holy Father, Everlasting God, Who has condescended, not for any merits of mine, but of Thy great mercy only, to feed me a sinner, Thine unworthy servant, with the precious Body and Blood of Thy Son, our Lord Jesus Christ; and I pray that this Holy Communion may not be for my judgment and condemnation, but for my pardon and salvation.

Let it be unto me an armour of faith and a shield of good purpose, a riddance of all vices, and a rooting out of all evil desires; an increase of love and patience, of humility and obedience, and of all virtues; a firm defence against the wiles of all my enemies, visible and invisible; a perfect quieting of all my evil impulses, fleshly and spiritual; a cleaving unto Thee, the one true God; and a blessed consummation of my end when Thou dost call.

And I pray that Thou wouldst bring me, a sinner, to that unspeakable Feast where Thou, with Thy Son and Thy Holy Spirit, art to Thy holy ones true light, fulness and blessedness, everlasting joy, and perfect happiness. Through the same Christ our Lord.

St Thomas Aquinas

*Glory be to the Father, and to the Son,
and to the Holy Spirit.*

PRAYER TO THE BLESSED TRINITY

Eternal Father, I thank Thee for the gift that Thou hast given me. It is Thy beloved Son, in whom Thou art well pleased. In Him and by Him give me strength to keep all my good resolutions.

Eternal Son, I thank Thee for the gift that Thou hast given me. It is Thyself who didst die for me. Make me, dear Jesus, wiser with Thy heavenly wisdom, and show me clearly all the things I should do for God.

Eternal Spirit, I thank Thee for the gift that Thou hast given me. It is Jesus, whose Soul Thou didst sanctify with Thy holiest treasures. Make me, dear Spirit, more loving that I may cling more closely to God.

O Ever-blessed Trinity, Three Persons and One God, help me to live according to this gift of gifts which I have received at the Altar of Jesus.

Anon

INTERIOR SILENCE

When last you went to Communion, what were the dispositions of your heart as the bell tinkled in the sanctuary? Were you waiting for Him like the shepherds of Bethlehem; were you keeping watch, as they were, over your thoughts, as they over their flocks, so that you were ready for His coming? Or was your heart like the wayside inn, too full of other guests to give a thought to His miraculous birth?

When we make our preparation for Communion, there should be a silence as of midnight in our hearts; not a feverish activity of aspirations and petitions, but an interior silence that banishes from the mind the busy echoes of its daily preoccupations; those plans we were forming, those grudges we were nursing, those anxieties we were harbouring, those fears we were encouraging - well, perhaps it is too much to ask that we should banish them altogether, but they should be hushed, as men's footsteps are hushed outside the door of a sick-room.

It is in the silence of the heart that we shall hear that whisper, *Hoc est Corpus meum,* and know that Christ is born.

But if our Lord's Presence in the Holy Eucharist means a birth, it also means a marriage; the moment at which we receive the Blessed Sacrament is the moment at which He plights His love to us in a supreme manner, making us one with Himself... Just in that moment, we want to be all for Him, *dilectus meus mihi, et ego illi* (my Beloved for me, and I for Him); that is the good part surely, which shall not be taken away from us.

R.A. Knox
The Window in the Wall

Let them bring me to Your holy mountain
to the place where You dwell. (Ps 42:3)

ODE TO CHRIST THE SAVIOUR

Christ incarnate makes me worthy of God,
Christ humbled for me, raises me high,
Christ, the giver of life,
suffering in human nature,
makes me impassive.
And so, I sing a hymn of thanksgiving,
to Him who is glorified.

Christ crucified raises me high,
Christ who is slain makes me rise again with Him;
Christ gives me life.
And so, clapping my hands with joy,
I sing to the saviour a hymn of victory,
to Him who is glorified.

Cosmas of Maiuma
in *Hymns to Christ*

THE GRACES OF HOLY COMMUNION

All the graces bestowed on our Blessed Lady and the saints, all the visions and ecstasies and the power of working miracles, are not to be compared in value with what He gives us in Holy Communion; for that is Himself. This gift which is Himself, is not for the few, but for everybody. *O res mirabilis, manducat Dominum pauper, servus et humilis:* we are all paupers in His sight, all slaves, creatures of earth, and He will make no distinctions between us. He only asks that we should purge our consciences of mortal sin, and so come to Him, asking Him to bring just what He wants to give us, just what He knows we need. "I am He Who bade this be done; I will supply what is lacking to thee; come, and receive Me."

R.A. Knox
The Window in the Wall

THE PLEDGE OF OUR RESURRECTION

Those who feed on Christ in the Eucharist need not wait until the hereafter to receive eternal life: they already possess it on earth, as the first-fruits of a future fullness which will embrace man in his totality. For in the Eucharist we also receive the pledge of our bodily resurrection at the end of the world: *"He who eats My flesh and drinks My blood has eternal life, and I will raise him up at the last day"* (Jn 6:54). This pledge of the future resurrection comes from the fact that the flesh of the Son of Man, given as food, is His body in its glorious state after the resurrection. With the Eucharist we digest, as it were, the "secret" of the resurrection. For this reason Saint Ignatius of Antioch rightly defined the Eucharistic Bread as *"a medicine of immortality, an antidote to death"*.

Pope John Paul II
Ecclesia de Eucharistia, **2003**

Let the heavens and the earth give Him praise. (Ps 68:35)

PRAYER OF PRAISE

Strengthen, O Lord, the hands which are stretched out to receive the Holy Things, that they may daily bring forth the fruit of good works. Grant, O my Lord, that the lips that praise Thee may be worthy to sing to Thy praise in Thy temple, and glorify Thee for ever; that the ears which have heard the sound of Thy canticles may never listen to the noise of fear and dissension; that the eyes which have seen Thy great love may also behold Thy blessed hope; that the tongues which have sung Holy, Holy, Holy, may speak truth; that the feet which have walked in the church may tread in the place of light; and that the bodies which have fed upon Thy living Body may be restored in newness of life.

Let Thine help come upon this congregation and let Thy fathomless love remain with us; may we more widely shew forth Thy glory, Whose divinity we worship, and may a door be opened to the prayers of us all. By the gift of the grace of the Holy Ghost we have been enabled to draw near and become fellow-partakers in these most excellent, holy, divine and life-giving mysteries; let us praise and rejoice in God, Who gave them.

From the Malabar Liturgy

We have been filled with grace, O Lord,
who have tasted Thy Body and Blood.
Glory in the highest be unto that Providence
which always feeds us.
Send down upon us Thy spiritual blessings.
Glory in the highest be unto Him Who provideth for us.

Armenian Liturgy
Ancient Devotions for Holy Communion

THE EUCHARIST ENKINDLES CHARITY

As bodily nourishment restores lost strength, so the Eucharist strengthens our charity, which tends to be weakened in daily life; and this living charity wipes away venial sins. By giving Himself to us Christ revives our love and enables us to break our disordered attachments to creatures and root ourselves in Him:

> Since Christ died for us out of love, when we celebrate the memorial of His death at the moment of sacrifice we ask that love may be granted to us by the coming of the Holy Spirit. We humbly pray that in the strength of this love by which Christ willed to die for us, we, by receiving the gift of the Holy Spirit, may be able to consider the world as crucified for us, and to be ourselves as crucified to the world ... Having received the gift of love, let us die to sin and live for God.[1]

Catechism of the Catholic Church
Para 1394

By the same charity that it enkindles in us, the Eucharist preserves us from future mortal sins. The more we share the life of Christ and progress in His friendship, the more difficult it is to break away from Him by mortal sin. The Eucharist is not ordered to the forgiveness of mortal sins; that is proper to the sacrament of Reconciliation. The Eucharist is properly the sacrament of those who are in full communion with the Church.

Ibid, Para 1395

---

1. St Fulgentius of Ruspe

*God is love, and he who abides in love
abides in God, and God abides in him.* (1 Jn 4:16)

PRAYER FROM THE BYZANTINE LITURGY

O our God, Divine Redeemer, teach us Thyself to give Thee worthy thanks for all that Thou hast done and still dost do for us.

O our God, Who hast accepted these gifts, cleanse us from all impurity of body and of spirit and teach us to maintain holiness in Thy fear, that, receiving our portion of Thine holy gifts with a pure conscience, we may be made one with the holy Body and Blood of Thy Christ; that having received them worthily we may have Christ dwelling in our hearts and become the temple of Thine Holy Spirit.

Let not any one of us, O our God, receive the sentence of guilt or incur sickness of body or soul on account of unworthy participation in Thy terrible and heavenly Mysteries; but let us until our last breath fittingly receive our share of Thine holy things as food for our journey to everlasting life and as an acceptable plea before the mighty judgement-seat of Thy Christ; that we also, with all the holy ones who have been pleasing to Thee from the beginning of the world, may become sharers in the everlasting good things which Thou hast prepared, O Lord, for them that love Thee.

Amen.

Liturgy of St Basil

THE SACRED HEART OF JESUS

Do not worry about your faults, but when you have committed one, say quite confidently to the most loving Heart of Jesus: "O my only Love, pay Your poor slave's debts and make good the evil I have just done. Turn it to Your glory, the edification of the neighbour, and the salvation of my soul." In this way our falls sometimes help very much to humble us and to teach us what we really are; also how useful it is for us to remain hidden in the depths of our nothingness.

The Sacred Heart is an inexhaustible fountain of mercy. It seeks only to fill humble hearts, hearts emptied of self and bound down by nothing so that they may be ever ready to sacrifice themselves to His good pleasure, no matter how much it may cost nature.

For one cannot love without suffering. He showed us this very clearly upon the cross, where He was consumed for love of us. And it is still the same every day in the Blessed Sacrament of the altar. There He ardently desires that we conform our life to His, completely effaced and hidden away from the eyes of man. Since love makes lovers one in likeness, if we love, let us model our lives on His.

This is what I ask of Him for you. I wish you to belong completely to the loving Heart of Jesus, to live no longer but in Him, for Him and through Him.

St Margaret Mary Alacoque
Letters
Translated by Clarence Herbst SJ

*Where your treasure is,
there will your heart be also.*

(Lk 12:34)

CHRIST IN OUR HEARTS

Simeon gave back Jesus to His Mother, he was only suffered to keep Him for one moment. But we are far happier than Simeon. We may keep Him always if we will. In Communion He comes not only into our arms but into our hearts.

St John Vianney
Sermon on the Feast of the Purification

If you only knew how Jesus hungers for you, how He burns with desire to come into your heart, how impatient He is to come down to you, bridging all distance between you and Him!

The day you miss a Communion is a great disappointment for Him. So go to Him; respond to His desire. *"Desidero desideravi.* I have desired with a great desire to eat this Pasch with you. I thirst. I thirst for you to come to Me; I thirst to come down into you."

Never deprive Him of this happiness through your own fault ... give Him the joy of descending into your heart, which is a heaven for Him.

Père Jean du Coeur de Jésus d'Elbée
I Believe in Love

Our Lord comes into us sacramentally in order to live there spiritually.

St Peter Julian Eymard

Give life to my soul that I may praise You. (Ps 118:175)

FULLNESS OF JOY IN YOUR PRESENCE

Lord Jesus, make us Your witnesses.
Help us spread Your fragrance everywhere.
Flood our soul with Your spirit and life.
Penetrate and possess our whole being so utterly
that our whole life may be a witness, a radiance, of Yours.
Shine through us and be so in us
that every soul we come in contact with
may be aware of Your presence in us.
Let them look at us and see no longer us,
but only You, Lord Jesus.

John Henry Cardinal Newman

Make my soul Your throne, O unchanging One, O Holy Trinity.

Blessed Elizabeth of the Trinity

The Word through Whom was created the universe
has entered my soul.
My Jesus, You are enthroned within me.
I bow down in awe and adoration at such a profound mystery.

Anon

Heaven is God and God is in my soul.

Raoul Plus SJ
In Christ Jesus

INTIMACY WITH CHRIST

Contemplation prolongs Communion and enables one to meet Christ, true God and true man, in a lasting way, to let oneself be seen by Him and to experience His Presence. When we contemplate Him present in the Blessed Sacrament of the altar, Christ draws near to us and becomes more intimate to us than we are to ourselves.

Pope John Paul II
Letter to the Bishop of Liège, **Belgium, 1996**

*They recognised the Lord Jesus
by the breaking of the bread.* (Lk 24:30-31)

PRAYER OF PETITION

Cleanse my heart, O Holy Spirit, by this heavenly food,
wherein Jesus gives me Himself.
Strengthen my faith that I may see Jesus
in the Sacrament of His Body and Blood.

I have often to go my way
through darkness and many temptations,
but Thou art my light and my strength.

In Thee I trust; by Thy grace I can do all things
that Jesus wishes me to do.
Be ever in my soul as the dew of the night.

With utter trust I rest on Thee
and believe the testimony which Thou givest.
Set up more and more Thy kingdom in my soul.

Anon

ST THÉRÈSE'S SONG

You know how tiny I am,
Yet You are not afraid to bend down to me.
Come into my heart, O white Host that I love,
Come into my heart, it longs for You!
Ah! I wish that Your goodness
Would let me die of love after this favour.
Jesus! Hear the cry of my tender feeling.
Come into my heart!
Come into my heart!

**St Thérèse of Lisieux
Translated by Fiona McAlpine, 2002
for Launceston Carmel**

CHRIST OUR LOVE

I am betrothed to the One
Whom the angels, trembling,
Will serve for all eternity.
The moon and the sun tell His praises,
Admire His beauty.

St Thérèse of Lisieux
Extract from Les Répons de Sainte Agnès
Poésies
Translated by Audrey English

There is but one Lover of souls and He loves each one of us, as though there were no one else to love. He died for each one of us, as if there were no one else to die for. He died on the shameful cross. The love which He inspires lasts, for it is the love of the unchangeable. It satisfies, for He is inexhaustible. The nearer we draw to Him, the more triumphantly does He enter into us; the longer He dwells in us, the more intimately have we possession of Him. It is an espousal for eternity.

John Henry Cardinal Newman
Callista

Jesus! I would so love Him!
Love Him as never yet He has been loved.

St Thérèse of Lisieux
IV Letter to Mother Agnes of Jesus
(Her sister, Pauline)
Thoughts of St Thérèse

I rejoiced to do Your will as though all riches were mine. (Ps 118:14)

LAUDA SION SALVATOREM

Laud, O Sion, Thy Salvation,
Laud, with hymns of exultation,
Christ, thy King and Shepherd true,
Bring Him all the praise thou knowest,
He is more than thou bestowest,
Never canst thou reach His due.

Special theme for glad thanksgiving
Is the Living and Lifegiving
Bread, today before thee set,
From His hands of old partaken,
As we know by faith unshaken,
Where the Twelve at supper met.

Full and clear ring out thy chanting,
Joy nor sweetest grace be wanting,
From thy heart let praises burst,
For today the Feast is holden
When the Institution olden
Of that Supper is rehearsed.

Here the new law's new oblation,
By the new King's revelation,
Ends the form of ancient rite,
Now the New the old effaces,
Truth away the shadow chases,
Light dispels the gloom of night.

What He did, at the supper seated,
Christ ordained to be repeated,
His Memorial ne'er to cease,
And His rule for guidance taking,
Bread and Wine we hallow, making
Thus our Sacrifice of peace.

Wondrous truth by Christians learnèd,
Bread into His Flesh is turnèd,
Into precious Blood the Wine,
Sight hath failed, nor thought conceiveth,
But a dauntless faith believeth,
Resting on a Power Divine.

Here beneath these signs are hidden
Priceless things, to sense forbidden,
Signs, not things, are all we see -
Flesh from bread, and Blood from wine,
Yet is Christ in either sign,
All entire confessed to be.

Whose of this Food partaketh
Rendeth not the Lord, nor breaketh,
Christ is whole to all that taste,
Thousands are, as one, receivers,
One, as thousands of believers,
Eats of Him Who cannot waste.

Bad and good the Feast are sharing,
O what diverse dooms preparing,
Endless death or endless life!
Life to these, to those damnation,
See how like participation
Is with unlike issues rife.

When the Sacrament is broken,
Doubt not, but believe 'tis spoken,
That each severed outward token
Doth the very Whole contain,
Naught the precious Gift divideth,
Breaking but the sign betideth,
Jesus still the same abideth,
Still unbroken doth remain.

Lo, the Angels' Food is given
To the pilgrim who hath striven,
See the children's Bread from Heaven
Which on dogs may ne'er be spent,
Truth the ancient types fulfilling,
Isaac bound a victim willing,
Paschal Lamb its Life Blood spilling,
Manna to the Fathers sent.

Very Bread, Good Shepherd, tend us,
Jesu, of Thy love befriend us;
Thou refresh us, Thou defend us,
Thine eternal goodness send us
In the Land of life to see,
Thou who all things canst and knowest
Who on earth such Food bestowest.
Grant us with Thy Saints, though lowest,
Where the Heavenly Feast Thou showest,
Fellow-heirs and guests to be.

Amen.

St Thomas Aquinas

FREQUENT AND DAILY COMMUNION

Since it is clear that the frequent or daily reception of the Blessed Eucharist increases union with Christ, nourishes the spiritual life more abundantly, strengthens the soul in virtue and gives the communicant a stronger pledge of eternal happiness, parish priests, confessors and preachers will frequently and zealously exhort the Christian people to this holy and salutary practice.[1]

Eucharisticum Mysterium
Sacred Congregation of Rites, 1967

1. Decree on the Daily Reception of Communion.

Whoever wants to persevere, let him receive Our Lord. He is the Bread that will nourish your failing strength, that will sustain you. The Church wants it this way. She encourages daily Communion. Holy Communion should be, above all, the aim of Christian life. Every pious exercise that does not have some relationship with Holy Communion is not directed towards its main goal.

St Peter Julian Eymard

One's everyday life ought to be both a preparation and a thanksgiving for Communion.

St John Vianney
On Communion

Where your treasure is, there will your heart be also. (Lk 12:34)

PRAYER FOR FOSTERING THE PRACTICE OF DAILY COMMUNION

O sweetest Jesu, Thou who camest into the world to give all souls the life of Thy grace, and Who, to preserve and nourish it in them, hast willed to be at once the daily cure of their daily infirmities and their daily sustenance, we humbly beseech Thee, by Thy Heart all on fire with love for us, to pour forth upon them all Thy divine Spirit, so that those who are unhappily in mortal sin, may turn to Thee and regain the life of grace which they have lost, and those who, through Thy gift, are already living this divine life, may draw near daily, when they can, to Thy sacred table, whence, by means of daily Communion, they may receive daily the antidote of their daily venial sins, and may every day foster within themselves the life of grace; and being thus ever more and more purified, may come at last to the possession of that eternal life which is happiness with Thee.

Amen.

The Raccolta

THE UNITY OF THE MYSTICAL BODY

Those who receive the Eucharist are united more closely to Christ. Through it Christ unites them to all the faithful in one body, the Church. Communion renews, strengthens, and deepens this incorporation into the Church, already achieved by Baptism. In Baptism we have been called to form but one body. The Eucharist fulfills this call: "The cup of blessing which we bless, is it not a participation in the Blood of Christ? The Bread which we break, is it not a participation in the Body of Christ? Because there is one Bread, we who are many are one body, for we all partake of the one Bread":

> *If you are the body and members of Christ, then it is your Sacrament that is placed on the table of the Lord; it is your Sacrament that you receive. To that which you are you respond "Amen" ("yes, it is true!") and by responding to it you assent to it. For you hear the words, "The Body of Christ" and respond "Amen". Be then a member of the Body of Christ that your "Amen" may be true.[1]*

Catechism of the Catholic Church
Para 1396

The gift of Christ and His Spirit which we receive in Eucharistic communion superabundantly fulfils the yearning for fraternal unity deeply rooted in the human heart; at the same time it elevates the experience of fraternity already present in our common sharing at the same Eucharistic table to a degree which far surpasses that of the simple human experience of sharing a meal. Through her communion with the body of Christ the Church comes to be ever more profoundly *"in Christ in the nature of a sacrament, that is, a sign and instrument of intimate unity with God and of the unity of the whole human race"*[2].

Pope John Paul II
***Ecclesia de Eucharistia*, 2003**

1. St Augustine
2. Documents of Vatican Council II, *Lumen Gentium,* 1963

Abide in Me, and I will in you. (Jn 15:14)

THANKSGIVING AFTER COMMUNION

May Thy holy Body, O Lord Jesus Christ our God, be to me eternal life, and Thy precious Blood to the remission of sins; and may this Eucharist be to me joy, health and gladness. And at Thy terrible second coming grant that I, a sinner, may stand at the right hand of Thy glory, through the prayers of Thy most pure Mother, and of all the Saints.

COPTIC LITURGY OF ST BASIL

Our mouths are filled with joy and our tongues with exultation, because we are made partakers, O Lord, of Thine immortal Sacrament; because the things which eye hath not seen, nor ear heard, neither hath it entered into the heart of man to conceive, Thou hast revealed to those that love Thy Name, and to the little ones of Thy holy Church.

Even so, Father, for so it seemed good in Thy sight; for Thou art merciful; and to Thee we ascribe glory, honour, and adoration, Father, Son, and Holy Ghost, now and ever, and to all ages,

Amen.

Ancient Devotions for Holy Communion

THE VALUE OF PRIVATE PRAYER

The divine Redeemer holds in close union with Himself not only His Church, as His beloved Bride, but in her also the souls of each one of the faithful, with whom He ardently desires to have intimate converse, especially after they have received Holy Communion. And although public prayer, as proceeding from Mother Church herself, excels beyond any other by reason of the dignity of the Bride of Christ, nevertheless all prayers, even those said in the most private way, have their dignity and their efficacy, and are also of great benefit to the whole mystical Body; for in that Body there can be no good and virtuous deed performed by individual members which does not, through the Communion of Saints, redound also to the welfare of all.

Pope Pius XII
Mystici Corporis, **1943**

Lord, make me know Your ways.
Lord, teach me Your paths. (Ps 24:4)

CONVERSION OF HEART

Too late have I known Thee, O ancient truth! Too late have I loved Thee, O Beauty ever ancient and ever new! And behold Thou wast within, and I was abroad, and there I sought Thee, and, deformed as I was, ran after those beauties which Thou hast made.

Thou wast with me and I was not with Thee; those things kept me far from Thee, which could have no being but in Thee.

Thou hast called, Thou hast cried out, and hast pierced my deafness and dispersed my blindness. Thou hast sent forth Thy fragrance and I have drawn my breath, and pant after Thee, and hunger after Thee.

I have tasted Thee, and I hunger and thirst after Thee. Thou hast touched me, and I have burned for Thy peace.

St Augustine of Hippo
The Confessions

SHARING THE LIFE OF GRACE

The fact that the sacred function, liturgically considered, has come to an end, does not dispense him who has communicated from making his thanksgiving. On the contrary, it is most seemly that after he has received Holy Communion, and after the Mass is over, he should collect his thoughts and, in close union with his divine Master, pass such time as circumstances allow in devout and salutary converse with Him.

The Divine Redeemer loves to listen to our entreaties, to speak with us familiarly, and to give us a refuge in His Heart which burns with love for us.

Indeed, these acts of private devotion are quite necessary if we are to receive in abundance the supernatural treasures in which the Eucharist is so rich, and to pour them out upon others, according to our powers, in order that Christ our Lord may reach the fullness of His power in the souls of all.

Pope Pius XII
***Mediator Dei*, 1947**

*The Lord will give strength to His people,
the Lord will bless His people with peace.* (Ps 28:11)

PRAYER OF THANKSGIVING

O Spirit of the Father and the Son, in the dawn of the world Thou didst move over the face of the waters. Thou didst overshadow the Mother of God in Nazareth, when the Word was made flesh, and God sent forth His Son made of a woman. Thou art He by Whom Jesus offered Himself without spot to God on the Altar of the Cross. By Thee Jesus is offered now in this unbloody Sacrifice of the Altar.

Thou art the Sanctifier, Almighty and Eternal God, and Thou dost ever bless the Sacrifice that is made ready for Thy name. O loving Spirit, strengthen my faith. Give me an ever-brighter love for Jesus. He is Emmanuel, God with us: God with us in our human nature, God with us in this Sacrament of His love.

Dear Spirit, I live and move and am in Thee: and I love Thee.

Anon

*By this all men will know
that you are My disciples,
if you have love for one another.*

(Jn 13:35)

Love one another as I have loved you. (Jn 15:12)

ANCIENT EUCHARISTIC PRAYER

Let us invoke Christ.
The sacred Body of Christ!
The Lamb of God,
the sacred Body of Him
Who died for our salvation!

The sacred Body of Him
Who revealed the mystery of grace
of the new covenant
to His disciples.

The sacred Body
Which washed with water
the feet of the apostles,
and with the Spirit
washed their souls.

The sacred Body
Which pardoned the penitent woman;
the sacred Body
Whose Blood makes us clean.

The sacred Body
Which received the kiss of betrayal;
the sacred Body
Which loved the world so much
as to accept even death on a cross.

We bless and glorify Your name.

from *Hymns to Christ*

A PRAYER BEFORE A PICTURE OF CHRIST

Most merciful God, let me ardently desire what pleases You, prudently seek, truly learn, and faithfully fulfil all to the praise and glory of Your name. Order my day so that I may know what You want me to do, and for my soul's good, help me to do it.

Let me not be elated by success nor cast down by failure, neither puffed up by the former, nor depressed by the latter. I want only to take pleasure in what draws me to You, only to grieve for what displeases You.

I want neither to please nor fear to displease anyone but You. For love of the eternal I would forgo the things of time. May all the joys in which You have no part weary me.

Work done for You is pleasure, relaxation apart from You, tedium. Teach me to turn my thoughts to You often and with firm purpose of amendment to feel contrite when I have failed to do so.

Make me obedient without cavil, poor without repining, pure without corruption, patient without murmuring, humble without pretence, cheerful without dissipation, sorrowful without dejection, serious without solemnity, gay without levity, truthful without deceit.

Let me fear You without despairing, do good without presuming, correct my neighbour without arrogance, edify him by word and action without hypocrisy.

Give me, O Lord, a vigilant heart lest vain thoughts take me from You, a noble heart that no unworthy affection can debase, an upright heart that no bad intention can degrade. Give me a strength that will withstand any trial, a liberty of spirit that no violent passion can overcome.

Grant me, O Lord my God, a mind to know You, a heart to seek You, wisdom to find You, conduct pleasing to You, faithful perseverance in waiting for You, and a hope of finally embracing You.

Here I accept trials as penance, your favours as grace for the way, Your joys especially as pledge of glory in heaven.

St Thomas Aquinas

PETITION

O Ever-blessed Trinity, One God, Thou hast given me bread in my hunger and drink in my thirst. I call to mind all Thy love and gentleness and compassion, in which Thou hast led me and guided me until now. With all my heart I pray for greater gifts of Thy grace and more overflowing treasure of Thy love.

Dwell in me more and more, as the Lord of the harvest and the vintage, that I may wash my robe in wine and my raiment in the blood of the grape. Give to me, as Thou only canst give, the blessings of heaven above, and the blessings of the deep that lieth beneath.

In the morning let me rise with Thee in faithfulness, that in the evening I may rest safely with Thee in love and joy and peace. O God, my soul resteth in Thee.

Anon

ODE TO CHRIST CRUCIFIED

By the tree of the cross
You have healed the bitterness of the tree,
And have opened Paradise to me.
Glory be to You, Lord!
Now we are no longer prevented
From coming to the tree of life;
We have hope in Your cross.
Glory be to You, Lord!

O Immortal One, nailed to the wood,
You have triumphed over the snares of the devil.
Glory be to You, Lord!

You, Who for my sake
Have submitted
To being placed on the cross,
Accept my vigilant celebration of praise,
O Christ, God, Friend of men.

Lord of the heavenly armies,
Who know my carelessness of soul,
Save me by Your cross,
O Christ, God, Friend of men.

Brighter than fire, more luminous than flame,
Have You shown the wood of Your cross, O Christ.
Burn away the sins of the sick
And enlighten the hearts of those who with hymns
Celebrate Your voluntary crucifixion.
Christ, God, glory to You!

Christ, God,
Who for us accepted
A sorrowful crucifixion,
Accept all who sing hymns to Your passion,
And save us.

**Byzantine liturgy
in *Hymns to Christ***

COMMUNION CHANT

Your sacrament, Lord Jesus Christ,
gives life
and the remission of sins;
You have suffered the passion for our sake.

For us You have drunk gall
to take from us all bitterness;

You have drunk a bitter wine for us
to lift us from our weariness;

You have been despised for us,
that the dew of immortality
might be poured upon us;

You have been beaten with scourges
to ensure to our frailty eternal life;

You have been crowned with thorns
that Your faithful might be crowned
with the evergreen laurels of love;

You have been wrapped in a winding sheet
that we might be clothed in Your strength;

You were laid in the tomb
that in a new age loving kindness
might again be granted to us.

**Fragment from an ancient Eucharistic liturgy
in *Hymns to Christ***

In Your great love, answer me, O God. (Ps 68:14)

PLEA FOR PROTECTION

With the seal of the cross,
impressed with Your blood,
with which we have been baptized
to make us ready for adoption,
You have modelled us into the image of Your glory.
By all these divine gifts,
Satan be put to confusion, his plots overturned,
his snares evaded, the enemy vanquished,
his sharp weapons repelled,
light shine through the gloom,
darkness be dispelled,
mists fade away.
Would that Your arms might receive us
into Your protection,
Your right hand press its seal upon us.
You are indeed full of love and clemency
and Your name is invoked over Your faithful.
To You, together with the Father,
through the Holy Spirit,
be glory and majesty through all ages.

Amen.

St Gregory of Narek
in *Hymns to Christ*

CANTICLE FOR THE EASTER VIGIL

Today we have contemplated upon the altar
our Lord Jesus Christ ...
Today we have heard His voice,
powerful yet gentle,
admonishing us;

This is the Body Which burns up
the thorns of sin
and gives light to the souls of men ...
This is the Body in Whose presence
the daughter of the Canaanite was cured.
This is the Body, Which, approached
in full confidence by the sinful woman,
set her free from the mire of sin.
This is the Body Thomas touched
and recognising, cried out:
my Lord and my God.
This is the Body, great and most high,
Which is the principle of our salvation.

One day He Who is the Word and our Life
determined that His blood
should be poured out for us
and offered for the forgiveness of our sins.

We have drunk of the Blood
by Which we have been redeemed,
restored, instructed, given light.

Who is entitled to celebrate
the mystery of grace?
We have been found worthy
to share in this gift.
Let us keep it to the end that we may hear
from His holy and blessed voice:

*"Come, O blessed, to My Father,
receive the inheritance
of the kingdom prepared for you."*

Then those who crucified the Lord will fear;
those who have not believed
in the Father, Son and Holy Spirit will be ashamed;
those who have denied and not borne witness
to the most holy Trinity, one God, will be lost.

As for us, beloved,
we celebrate the wonder of the baptism of Jesus,
His holy and life-giving resurrection,
through which salvation has come to the world.
We await the happy fulfilment of redemption
in the grace and love of our Lord Jesus Christ,
to Whom is due all glory, honour and adoration.

**Fragment from an ancient Eucharistic liturgy
in *Hymns to Christ***

May Your glory shine on earth! (Ps 56:6)

EASTER HYMN

We glorify You, O Christ, singing:
glory to the Lord!
He was born of the Holy Spirit
in order to give us life.
He deigned to dwell among us.
To Him we render our veneration,
crying out together:
Glory to the Lord!

Behold: the Virgin has given birth to Emmanuel.
He has come down from heaven,
has saved from Egypt a people that was lost.
Let us exalt Him, crying:
Glory to the Lord!

He has willed to overcome our enemy;
has made His dwelling in the Virgin Mary:
the invisible has become visible in flesh.
Let us adore Him, crying out:
Glory to the Lord!

Born of a woman ever virgin,
the Word of truth rose again for us.
Let us celebrate the Lord, intoning:
Glory to the Lord!

Light from light, Christ our King
is risen for us.
He has saved us from the land of Egypt;
all together let us sing:
Glory to the Lord!

**Fragment from an ancient Eucharistic liturgy
in *Hymns to Christ***

*While He blessed them, He parted from them,
and was carried up into heaven.* (Lk 24:51)

HYMN FOR ASCENSION DAY

On this day the new Bread of the spirit has gone up to heaven.
The mysteries were revealed in Your Body
Which has gone up as an offering.
Blessed be Your Bread, O Lord!

The Lamb has come to us from the house of David;
the Priest, from the stock of Abraham,
has become for our sakes the Lamb of God,
the new minister of sacrifice.

His Body is the victim, His Blood is our drink.
Blessed be the new sacrifice!

He has descended from heaven like the light;
is born of Mary as a divine shoot;
as a fruit He has fallen from the cross;
and is offered up to heaven as the first fruits.
Blessed be His will!

You are the offering of heaven and of earth,
immolated and at the same time adored.
You came to be a victim,
You ascended as a singular offering,
You ascended, Lord,
bearing with You the offering of Your sacrifice.

**St Ephrem of Syria
in *Hymns to Christ***

SPIRITUAL COMMUNION

Spiritual Communion is the heartfelt desire to receive Our Lord, even when we are unable because of distance or some other reason. This desire to receive Him through spiritual Communion is an act of love which prolongs our thanksgiving even when we are not in the Eucharistic presence of Our Lord.

The wish to live constantly in His presence can be fuelled by acts of love and desire to be united with Him and is a means of drawing more deeply from the life of the Holy Spirit dwelling within our souls in the state of grace.

The writings of the saints reveal many formulae for making a spiritual communion.

My Jesus, I believe that Thou art truly present in the Most Holy Sacrament. I love Thee above all things, and I desire to possess Thee within my soul Since I am unable now to receive Thee sacramentally, come at least spiritually into my heart. I embrace Thee as being already there, and unite myself wholly to Thee; never permit me to be separated from Thee.

St Alphonsus Liguori
The Holy Eucharist

I wish, my Lord, to receive You with the purity, humility and devotion with which Your Most Holy Mother received You, with the spirit and fervour of the saints.

COME, LORD JESUS.

If any man thirst, let him come to Me. (Jn 7:31)

SPIRITUAL COMMUNION PRAYER

I thank Thee, dear Jesus, for all Thy Sacraments. I thank Thee above all for Thyself. I thank Thee because I can feed upon Thee spiritually, even when I cannot come before Thy Altar. Give me a greater thirst for Thee, Thou lover of my soul, and let me sit beneath Thy shadow and taste of Thy sweetness more. Lift me to Thyself on high, and let my soul be steeped in Thy light.

Give me a great love for all things holy and just and pure and lovely and true. Let me feed on the pleasures of Thy right hand, and let me drink of the torrent of Thy river. Thy land is ever flowing with milk and honey; but Thou, my own Jesus, my loved One, art far sweeter than honey and the honeycomb.

Thy city has gates of pearl, and its jasper wall has foundations of precious stones; but Thou art the one Pearl without price, and for Thy love I would gladly sell all that I have. Thy sweetness deadens my taste for the world's gifts, and in all bitterness of sorrow the light of Thy face and the love of Thy heart are joy and rest and peace.

I bless and praise Thee for forgiving my sins. I bless and praise Thee for saving me from the undying fire. I bless and praise Thee for all Thy spiritual gifts here, and for the hope of Thy heavenly joys hereafter. Thou art my Jesus in Heaven and my Jesus on the Altar. Thou art my Jesus in my heart. For this I love Thee, and bless Thee, and praise Thee, and glorify Thee, and adore Thee for ever and ever.

Anon

SACRAMENTAL AND SPIRITUAL COMMUNION

The effects of a Sacrament can be received by desire, although in such a case the Sacrament is not received physically. Just as some are baptised by a Baptism of desire, as they had the desire for Baptism before they were baptised in water, so some receive the Eucharist spiritually before they eat sacramentally. However, the actual reception of the Sacrament itself has a fuller effect than receiving the Sacrament through desire alone.

St Thomas Aquinas
***Summa Theologica:* III, Q.80, a.1, ad 3**

If we loved Our Lord, we should have the Tabernacle, that dwelling place of God, always before the eyes of our mind.

St John Vianney
Thoughts of the Curé D'Ars

With discerning faith a distinguished writer of the Byzantine tradition voiced this truth: in the Eucharist *"unlike any other sacrament, the mystery [of communion] is so perfect that it brings us to the heights of every good thing: here is the ultimate goal of every human desire, because here we attain God and God joins Himself to us in the most perfect union"*[1].

Precisely, for this reason it is good to cultivate in our hearts a constant desire for the sacrament of the Eucharist. This was the origin of the practice of "spiritual communion", which has happily been established in the Church for centuries and recommended by saints who were masters of the spiritual life.

Pope John Paul II
***Ecclesia de Eucharistia*, 2003**

1. Nicolas Cabasilas, *Life in Christ*.

*With joy you will draw water
from the wells of salvation.* (Is 12:3)

PRAYERS OF LONGING

Give me, good Lord, a longing to be with Thee. Give me warmth, delight and quickness in thinking upon Thee. And give me Thy grace to long for Thine holy Sacraments, and specially to rejoice in the presence of Thy very blessed Body, Sweet Saviour Christ, in the Holy Sacrament of the altar.

St Thomas More

O God of love, my Saviour, my joy, my delight for eternity. Thou alone canst quench my thirst, and satiate my soul. Yet the more I feed on Thee, the more I hunger, the more I drink of Thy source, the more I thirst. Come, then, Lord Jesus, come.

St Gertrude

Give me the grace, dear Lord, to make
every step an act of faith in You,
every heartbeat an act of love for You,
every breath an act of longing for You.

Anon

PRIVATE PRAYER AFTER COMMUNION

On those who receive the Body and Blood of Christ, the gift of the Spirit is poured out abundantly like living water (cf. Jn 7:37-39), provided that this Body and Blood have been received sacramentally and spiritually, namely, by that faith which operates through charity.[1]

But union with Christ, to which the sacrament itself is directed, is not to be limited to the duration of the celebration of the Eucharist; it is to be prolonged into the entire Christian life, in such a way that the Christian faithful, contemplating unceasingly the gift they have received, may make their life a continual thanksgiving under the guidance of the Holy Spirit and may produce fruits of greater charity.

In order to remain more easily in this thanksgiving which is offered to God in an eminent way in the Mass, those who have been nourished by Holy Communion should be encouraged to remain for a while in prayer.[2]

Eucharisticum Mysterium
Sacred Congregation of Rites, 1967

1. Cf. Council of Trent, *Decree on the Eucharist*

2. Cf. Pope Pius XII, Encyclical Letter *Mediator Dei* (1947)

You shall love the Lord your God with all your heart. (Mt 22:37)

IN PRAISE OF GOD'S LOVE

O all powerful and eternal Trinity! O sweet and ineffable Charity, who would not be inflamed by so much love? What heart could refuse expending all for You?

O abyss of charity! You are so intensely attached to Your creatures that it would almost seem You cannot live without them! Yet You are God, having no need of us. Since You are unchangeable, our well-being adds nothing to Your greatness. Our wickedness causes You no harm since You are the sovereign and eternal Goodness. What is it that inspires You with such compassion?

It is love. For You have no obligation toward us, no need for us. What draws You then, O infinite God, to me Your puny creature?

It is nothing else than Yourself, Fire of Love! Love always, Love alone has impelled and still impels Your tenderness towards Your creatures, filling them with infinite graces and priceless gifts.

O Supreme Benevolence, You alone are supremely good! You have given us the Word, Your Son, to live with us, in touch with such corruption, such darkness. What is the cause of this gift?

Love! for You loved us before we even were.

O Eternal Magnificence! O Immensity of Goodness! You abased Yourself, becoming little, that man might become great. On whichever side I turn, I find only the abyss and fire of Your charity.

St Catherine of Siena

THANKSGIVING - A TREASURE OF GRACES

Immediately after Communion, the soul should spend time conversing with Jesus. The acts formed in prayer after Communion are far more precious and meritorious in the sight of God than when made at another time, for the soul being then united with Jesus, the value of the acts is increased by His presence. Moreover, after Communion, Jesus is more disposed to grant graces.

St Teresa says that after Communion Jesus remains in the soul as on a throne of grace and says: *"What do you want Me to do for you?"*[1], meaning: *"O soul, I have come for the express purpose of granting you graces. Ask Me what you will, as much as you will; you will receive all."*

O what treasures of grace would you receive, devout soul, if you only entertain yourself with Jesus for an hour, or at least half an hour, after Communion!

St Alphonsus Liguori
The Holy Eucharist

1. Mk 10:51

The Lord delights in you. (Is 62:4)

PRAYER

Come to me, life-giving Jesus, in Thy sweetness and might. Give me a greater longing for Thy gift of gifts. Satisfy my hunger with the Living Bread, and slake my thirst with the Wine of God.

Now I see Thee dimly in Thy creatures, and now darkly I know Thy love. I feel the wickedness of my heart, and am cast down greatly when I think of my unfaithfulness to Thee.

Purify me more and more, and cleanse me with the fire of Thy Heart. Wash me with Thy Precious Blood, and I shall be white; give me more of Thy Holy Spirit, and I shall be cleansed.

I adore Thee, Jesus, in the Blessed Sacrament, and with all my heart I wish to make myself a fitting temple for Thee. Come to me, O loving Jesus.

Anon

OUR LORD CHOOSES OUR HEARTS
AS HIS THRONE

The sole crime with which Herod reproached Our Lord was folly - and frankly that charge was true. Yes, it was folly to come seeking the poor shallow hearts of mortals, therein to make His throne. He, the King of Glory Who sitteth above the Cherubim! Was not His happiness complete in the company of His Father and the Spirit of Love? Why come to earth to seek out sinners and to make of them His friends, His chosen companions?

St Thérèse, *Thoughts of St Thérèse*
Letter to her sister, Céline

Oh! If we could rightly understand how Jesus Christ loves to come into our heart!

St John Vianney
Eucharistic Meditation, 10

O Lord my God, Father, Son, and Holy Spirit, make me ever to seek and love Thee, and by this Holy Communion which I have received, never to depart from Thee; for Thou art God, and beside Thee there is none else, for ever and ever.

Mozarabic Missal
Ancient Devotions for Holy Communion

6

For Children

Let the children come to Me

(Mk 10:14)

JESUS LOVES US

Some people brought children to Jesus, so that He might touch them. The disciples complained, but children are never a nuisance to Jesus and He said:

"Let the children come to Me".

Jesus always welcomes children. He loves them to visit Him in the church, where He lives in the tabernacle.

This is the amazing truth: Jesus, Who was born in Bethlehem 2000 years ago, is present in the Eucharist.

Every day at Mass, at the Consecration, the priest changes bread and wine into the Body and Blood of Jesus. If we are able, we receive Jesus in Holy Communion.

After Mass, the Sacred Hosts are placed in the tabernacle so that Jesus can be carried to the sick and so we can visit Him often.

Jesus gives Himself in the Eucharist because He loves us. He loves each one of us personally, when we are at home, when we are at school, when we are doing our chores, when we are studying and when we are playing.

Jesus loves us always, even when we disappoint Him. When we ask him for His mercy, Jesus always forgives us.

Jesus loves us so much that He died on the Cross to save us. He asks us to accept our daily crosses, to be obedient and kind, to be of service to others, to give our smile even when we are hurt or sad.

Jesus in the Eucharist should mean everything to us. When we go to Mass on Sundays and even during the week, when we pass the church on the way to and from school, Jesus is there in the Holy Eucharist.

He waits especially for His children, whom He loves so much.

*I am the Good Shepherd.
I know My sheep
and My sheep know Me.*

(Jn 10:14)

You are My friends. (Jn 15:14)

THE COMMANDMENT TO LOVE

This is My commandment,
that you love one another
as I have loved you.

Greater love has no man than this,
that a man lay down his life for his friends.
You are My friends
If you do what I command you.

I have called you friends,
for all that I have heard from My Father
I have made known to you.

(Jn 15:12-15)

Jesus is the greatest Friend you will ever have. Tell Him your secrets, tell Him your joys and the things that make you sad. Tell Him about the people whom you love.

**Pope John Paul II
to an Australian child preparing
for her First Holy Communion,
November 1986**

DAILY PRAYERS

The Sign of the Cross

In the name of the Father,
and of the Son,
and of the Holy Spirit. *Amen.*

Morning Offering

O Jesus, through the Immaculate Heart of Mary, I offer You all my prayers, works, joys and sufferings of this day in union with the holy Sacrifice of the Mass, for all the intentions of Your Divine Heart.

The Lord's Prayer

Our Father Who art in heaven,
Hallowed be Thy name,
Thy kingdom come,
Thy will be done on earth,
As it is in heaven.
Give us this day our daily bread.
And forgive us our trespasses,
As we forgive those who trespass against us.
And lead us not into temptation;
But deliver us from evil. *Amen.*

Prayer to the Blessed Trinity

Glory be to the Father, and to the Son, and to the Holy Spirit, as it was in the beginning, is now, and ever shall be, world without end. *Amen.*

Act of Contrition

O my God, I am very sorry that I have sinned against You, because You are so good, and with Your help, I will not sin again. *Amen.*

The Jesus Prayer

Lord Jesus Christ, Son of God,
have mercy on me, a sinner.

The Hail Mary

Hail Mary, full of grace, the Lord is with thee,
blessed art thou among women,
and blessed is the fruit of thy womb, Jesus.
Holy Mary, Mother of God, pray for us sinners,
now, and at the hour of our death. *Amen.*

Prayer to the Guardian Angel

Angel of God, my guardian dear,
to whom God's love commits me here,
ever this day be at my side,
to light and guard, to rule and guide. *Amen.*

JESUS TRANSFORMS US

A Little Host

The Holy Child does this for you:
That He may to your soul convey
His Life, as food! transforms - into
Himself - a little host, each day.
And (with a love that's greater still)
He wants to change *you also* - yes,
Into Himself! He longs to fill
Your heart - His joy, His happiness.
     Noël, Noël!
       I come here, to tell
You what will be for your delight
       The Lamb came to
        Be small, and to you!
Be, therefore, *His pure host of white!*

St Thérèse of Lisieux
The Divine Little Beggar-Boy of Christmas
Collected Poems of St Thérèse of Lisieux
(Gracewing, England)
Translated by Alan Bancroft

Come to Me. (Mt 11:28)

VISITING JESUS

When we come to the church, we make the Sign of the Cross with holy water. We genuflect to Jesus in the tabernacle and then we kneel down to pray quietly.

Jesus wants all of our attention. He loves us so much and He wants us to speak only to Him when we are in the church. It is the special place of His divine Presence. When we are very quiet, Jesus speaks to our souls in that beautiful silence.

As the priest changes the bread and wine into the Body and Blood of Jesus at Mass, Jesus changes us, little by little, into images of Himself when we receive Him in Communion and when we visit Him.

Jesus makes us holy. He wants us to be with Him in heaven forever.

PRAYER FOR A CHILD'S FIRST COMMUNION

Father, today, for the first time, You are calling our child ... to the table of the Eucharist. We ask that he/she may be a worthy member of Christ's mystical body, the Church. In the power of the Eucharist preserve ... from the assaults of evil, strengthen his/her faith, and make him/her a witness to Your love. Through Christ our Lord.

Amen.

Pope Paul VI
The Pope's Family Prayer Book

*My Flesh is food indeed and
My Blood is drink indeed* (Jn: 6:55)

PRAYER FOR FIRST COMMUNICANTS

O Jesus, Who hast loved us with such exceeding great love as to give us the ineffable gift of the Holy Eucharist, inflame us with the burning zeal to promote Thy glory by preparing worthily the little children who are to approach Thy holy table for the first time.

Protect, O Eucharistic Heart of Jesus, these young souls from the assaults of evil, strengthen their faith, increase their love and endow them with all the virtues that will make them worthy to receive Thee. Amen.

St John the Baptist, forerunner of the Messiah, prepare the way for Jesus in the hearts of these children.

Saint Tarcisius, keep safe the children who are making their first Communion.

The Raccolta
Approved by Pope Pius X, 1908

SIMPLE PRAYERS
BEFORE HOLY COMMUNION

Prayer for Help

O my God, help me to make a good Communion. Mary, my dearest mother, pray to Jesus for me. My dear angel guardian, lead me to the altar of God.

Act of Faith

O God, because You have said it, I believe that I shall receive the Sacred Body of Jesus Christ to eat, and His Precious Blood to drink. My God, I believe this with all my heart.

Act of Humility

My God, I confess that I am a poor sinner. I am not worthy to receive the Body and Blood of Jesus Christ on account of my sins. Lord, I am not worthy to receive You; only say the word and I shall be healed.

Act of Sorrow

My God, I detest all the sins of my life, I am sorry for them, because they have offended You, my God, Who are so good. I resolve never to commit sin any more. My good God, pity me, have mercy on me, forgive me.

Act of Adoration

O Jesus, great God, present on the Altar, I bow down before You, I adore You.

Act of Love and Desire

Sweet Jesus, I love You, I desire with all my heart to receive You. My most sweet Jesus, come into my poor soul, and give me Your flesh to eat and Your Blood to drink. Give me Your whole Self, Body, Blood, Soul, and Divinity, that I may live for ever with You.

AFTER HOLY COMMUNION

Act of Faith

O Jesus, I believe that I have received Your Flesh to eat and Your Blood to drink, because You have said it, and Your word is true.

Act of Adoration

O Jesus, my God, my Creator, I adore You, because from Your hands I came and with You I am to be happy for ever.

Act of Humility

O Jesus, I am but dust and ashes, and yet You have come to me, that my poor heart may speak to You.

Act of Love

Sweet Jesus, I love You. I love You with all my heart. You know that I love You, and wish to love You daily more and more.

Act of Thanksgiving

My good Jesus, I thank You with all my heart. How good, how kind You are to me, sweet Jesus. Blessed be Jesus in the most Holy Sacrament of the Altar.

Act of Offering

O Jesus, receive my poor offering. Jesus You have given Yourself to me, now let me give myself to You.

I give You my body that it may be chaste and pure. I give You my soul, that it may be free from sin.

I give You my heart, that it may always love You. I give You every breath that I shall breathe, and especially my last. I give You myself in life and in death, that I may be Yours for ever and ever.

Remember the words of Jesus,
"Ask and you shall receive."

PRAYER FOR YOURSELF

O Jesus, wash away my sins with Your Precious Blood.

O Jesus, the struggle against temptation is not yet finished. My Jesus, when temptation comes near me, make me strong against it. In the moment of temptation may I always say, *"Jesus, mercy!"* *"Mary, help!"*

O Jesus, may I lead a good life! May I die a happy death. May I receive You before I die. May I say when I am dying. *"Jesus, Mary, Joseph, I give you my heart and my soul."*

PRAYER FOR OTHERS

O Jesus, have mercy on Your Holy Church; take care of it. O Jesus, have pity on poor sinners, and save them from hell. O Jesus, bless my father, my mother, my brothers and sisters, and all I ought to pray for, as Your kind Heart knows how to bless them.

O Jesus, have pity on the poor souls burning in the flames of Purgatory, and give them eternal rest.

BEFORE LEAVING THE CHURCH

Sweet Jesus, I am going away for a time, but I trust not without You. You are with me by Your grace. I will never leave You by mortal sin. I do not fear to do so, though I am so weak, because I have such hope in You. Give me grace to persevere.

Amen.

The Holy Face
from the Shroud of Turin

I will walk in the way of perfection. (Ps 100:2)

ANIMA CHRISTI

Soul of Christ, sanctify me.
Body of Christ, save me.
Blood of Christ, refresh me.
Water flowing from the side of Christ, wash me.
Passion of Christ, strengthen me.
O good Jesus, hear me.
Within Thy wounds hide me.
Never permit me to be separated from Thee.
From the evil enemy, defend me.
At the hour of my death, call me.
And bid me to come to Thee,
That with Thy Saints, I may praise Thee,
For ever and ever,

Amen.

*In the presence of the angels
I will sing Your praise*

(Ps 138:1)

*There is no greater love than this:
to lay down one's life for one's friend.* (Jn 15:13)

PRAYER BEFORE A CRUCIFIX

Behold, O kind and most sweet Jesus, I cast myself upon my knees in Thy sight, and with the most fervent desire of my soul I pray and beseech Thee that Thou wouldst impress upon my heart lively sentiments of Faith, Hope, and Charity, with true repentance for my sins, and a firm desire of amendment, whilst with deep affection and grief of soul I ponder within myself and mentally contemplate Thy five most precious Wounds; having before my eyes that which David spoke in prophecy of Thee, O good Jesus: They have pierced my hands and feet; they have numbered all my bones.

A young girl receives her
First Holy Communion from the Holy Father
Mexico, January 1999.

MESSAGE TO CHILDREN

On the occasion of the festivity of Corpus Christi, on 14 June 1979, the Holy Father celebrated Mass in St Peter's Basilica. Over ten thousand children who had received First Communion in this period were present. An extract from Pope John Paul II's homily follows.

Beloved boys and girls!

You are the favourites of Jesus: *"Let the children come to Me!"*, the divine Master said, *"Do not hinder them!"* (Lk 18:16).

You are also my favourites!

Dear boys and girls! You prepared for your First Communion with such commitment and diligence, and your first meeting with Jesus was a moment of intense emotion and deep happiness. Remember for ever this blessed day of First Communion! Remember for ever your fervour and your pure joy!

Jesus is present with us.

This is the first thought.

Jesus rose again; He ascended to heaven: but He willed to remain with us and for us, in every place on earth. The Eucharist is really a divine invention!

Before dying on the Cross, offering His life to the Father as a sacrifice of adoration and love, Jesus instituted the Eucharist, changing the bread and the wine into His own Person and giving the Apostles and their successors, the Bishops and Priests, the power of making Him present in Holy Mass.

Jesus, therefore, willed to remain with us for ever! Jesus willed to be closely united with us in Holy Communion, to prove His love to us directly and personally. Each one can say: *"Jesus loves me! I love Jesus."*

St Thérèse of the Child Jesus, recalling the day of her First Communion, wrote: *"Oh, how sweet was the first kiss that Jesus gave my soul! ... It was a kiss of love, I felt loved and I said in my turn: 'I love You, I give myself to You for ever' ... Thérèse had disappeared like a drop of water lost in the ocean. There remained only Jesus: the master, the King."* (St Thérèse, Story of a Soul, Chapter 4). And she began to weep with joy and consolation, to the amazement of her companions.

Jesus is present in the Eucharist to be met, loved, received and consoled. Wherever there is the priest, Jesus is present, because the mission and greatness of the priest is precisely the celebration of Holy Mass.

Jesus is present in large cities and in little villages, in mountain churches and in the distant huts of Africa and Asia, in hospitals and prisons; Jesus in the Eucharist was even present in the concentration camps!

Dear children! Receive Jesus often! Abide in Him; let yourselves be transformed by Him!

Jesus is your greatest friend.

Here is the second thought.

Never forget it! Jesus wishes to be our closest friend, our companion along the way.

You have, certainly, so many friends, but you cannot always be with them and they cannot always help you, listen to you, console you.

Jesus, on the contrary, is the friend who never abandons you. Jesus knows you one by one, personally. He knows your name. He follows you, accompanies you, walks with you every day. He participates in your joys and consoles you in moments of grief and sadness. Jesus is the friend we cannot do without when we have met Him and understood that He loves us and wants our love.

You can speak and confide in Him; you can address Him with affection and confidence. Jesus even died on the cross for our sake! Make a pact of friendship with Jesus and never break it! In all the situations of your life, turn to the Divine Friend, present in us with His "Grace", present with us and in us in the Eucharist.

And be always messengers and joyful witnesses of your friend Jesus in your families, among your companions, in the places where you play and spend your holidays, in this modern society, so often so sad and dissatisfied.

Jesus is waiting for us.

Here is the last thought.

Life, long or short, is a journey towards Paradise; there is our fatherland, there is our real home; there is our appointment!

Jesus is waiting for us in Paradise! Never forget this supreme and consoling truth. And what is Holy Communion but an anticipation of Paradise? In fact, in the Eucharist it is Jesus Himself Who is waiting for us and Whom we will meet one day openly in Heaven.

Receive Jesus often in order never to forget Paradise, to be always on the march towards the house of the Heavenly Father, to enjoy Paradise a little already!

This was understood by Dominic Savio, who at the age of seven got permission to receive First Communion, and on that day wrote his resolutions:

"First: I will confess very often and I will receive Communion whenever the confessor gives me permission. Second: I wish to sanctify feast days. Third: my friends will be Jesus and Mary. Fourth: death rather than sin."

What little Dominic wrote so many years ago (in 1849) still holds good now and will hold good for ever.

Beloved boys and girls, I conclude by saying to you, keep yourselves worthy of Jesus Whom you receive!

Be innocent and generous! Undertake to make life beautiful for everyone with obedience, kindness, good manners! The secret of joy is goodness!

And to you, parents and relatives, I say anxiously and confidently: love your children, respect them, edify them! Be worthy of their innocence and of the mystery enclosed in their soul, created directly by God! They need love, delicacy, a good example, maturity! Do not neglect them! Do not betray them!

I entrust you all to Mary Most Holy, our Mother in heaven, the Star of the Sea of our life: pray to her every day, you children!

Give your hand to Mary Most Holy, so that she may lead you to receive Jesus in a holy way.

And let us also address a thought of affection and solidarity to all suffering children, to all boys and girls who cannot receive Jesus because they do not know Him, to all parents who have been tragically deprived of their children or are disappointed and grieved in their expectations.

*I entrust you all to Mary Most Holy,
our Mother in heaven,
the Star of the Sea of our life:
pray to her every day.*

(Pope John Paul II)

In your meeting with Jesus pray for everyone, commend everyone, invoke grace and assistance for everyone!

And pray also for me, you who are my favourites!

    Reprinted from L'Osservatore Romano English edition

A HEAVEN FOR JESUS

Here is a good thought which is not often mentioned: receive Communion not only for yourself, in order to have this immense grace, but for Jesus, in order to respond to His desire to come down into you, to give Him the joy of descending into your heart, which is a heaven for Him. Perhaps you will say, *"What? My poor heart, so miserable, so unworthy, a heaven for Jesus?"* Yes, if you call upon Him to make your heart a heaven for Him.

Listen to little Thérèse: *"I offered myself to Jesus, not as a person who desires to receive His visit for my own consolation, but on the contrary, for the pleasure of Him who gives Himself to me. It is not in order to remain in the golden ciborium that He comes down each day from Heaven, but in order to find another heaven, the heaven of our souls, made in His image, the living temple of the adorable Trinity."*[1]

Père Jean du Coeur de Jésus d'Elbée
I Believe in Love

1. *Manuscrits autobiographiques.*

7

Mary Our Mother

Blessed is the fruit of thy womb!

(Lk 1:42)

Behold your mother. (Jn 19:27)

AVE VERUM CORPUS, NATUM DE MARIA VIRGINE[1]

Let us invite the Blessed Virgin to preside maternally over the Eucharistic life of the entire Church. May she, the spouse of the Holy Spirit, implore from Him the attainment of that Life which Christ offers to all through the Sacrament of His Body and Blood, celebrated and received in the power of the Spirit of Life and Love.

Pope John Paul II
***Angelus Address*, Rome, 1986**

1. Hail, True Body, born of the Virgin Mary.

AVE VERUM CORPUS NATUM

Hail true Body, born of Mary,
Spotless Virgin's virgin birth;
Thou who truly hangest weary
On the Cross for sons of earth;
Then whose sacred side was riven,
Whence the water flowed and blood,
O may'st Thou, dear Lord, be given
At death's hour to be my food;
O most kind! O gracious One!
O sweetest Jesu, holy Mary's Son.

Ascribed to Pope Innocent VI, 1362
Translated by H.N. Oxenham

HOUSE OF GOLD

Mary is the house and the palace of the Great King, of God Himself. Our Lord, the co-equal Son of God, once dwelt in her. He was her guest; nay, more than a guest, for a guest comes into a house as well as leaves it. But Our Lord was actually born in this holy house.

He took His flesh and His blood from this house, from the flesh, from the veins of Mary. Rightly then was she made to be of pure gold, because she was to give of that gold to form the body of the Son of God. She was GOLDEN in her conception, GOLDEN in her birth. She went through the fire of her suffering, like gold in the furnace, and when she ascended on high, she was, in the words of our hymn,

> *Above all the Angels in glory untold,*
> *Standing next to the King in a vesture of gold.*

John Henry Cardinal Newman
Meditations on the Litany of Loreto

Blessed is the womb of the Virgin Mary,

She carried the Son of the eternal Father.

Communion Antiphon
The Roman Missal

My soul glorifies the Lord. (Lk 1:46)

PRAYER FROM THE LITURGY

You, Who once spoke to Moses
on Mount Sinai,
have received from an immaculate Virgin
flesh that is free from all sin.

You Who once pastured Israel,
now feed on the milk of a Mother
who has not known man.
O marvellous happening!

You Who once punished kings
now save Yourself from a king
by flight into Egypt.

You, seated in majesty [on a high throne]
were laid in a manger
retaining all Your dignity.

And now, full of faith,
we praise the Mother and sing to the Son.

He Who in heaven is God and has no mother,
has descended to earth and lived
as though motherless.

To You be the glory!

Fragment from an ancient Eucharistic liturgy
in *Hymns to Christ*

*The Word became flesh
and dwelt among us.*

(Jn 1:14)

He looks on His servant in her lowliness. (Lk 1:48)

ON HOLY COMMUNION

My God, who can be inhabited by Thee, except the pure and holy? Sinners may come to Thee, but to whom shouldst Thou come except to the sanctified?

My God, I adore Thee as the Holiest; and, when Thou didst come upon earth, Thou didst prepare a holy habitation for Thyself in the most chaste womb of the Blessed Virgin. Thou didst make a dwelling place special for Thyself. She did not receive Thee without first being prepared for Thee; for from the moment that she was at all, she was filled with Thy grace, so that she never knew sin. And so she went on increasing in grace and merit year after year, till the time came, when Thou didst send down the Archangel to signify to her Thy presence within her.

So holy must be the dwelling place of the Highest. I adore and glorify Thee, O Lord my God, for Thy great holiness.

John Henry Cardinal Newman
Meditations and Devotions

PRAYER TO OUR MOTHER

O my Mother! I never have a Communion but to thee I owe it. The tabernacle, the pyx, the monstrance - the very beauty of the mystery is that it is thy Jesus, and not another, the Body that was formed from thee, and not a new one, which consecration brings.

Frederick Faber
The Blessed Sacrament

WOMAN OF THE EUCHARIST

May the Queen of Apostles put her 'Magnificat' in your hearts every day and help you to translate it into a life that is always to the praise and glory of God.

Pope John Paul II
Moscow, June 1995

In a certain sense Mary lived her Eucharistic faith even before the institution of the Eucharist, by the very fact that she offered her virginal womb for the Incarnation of God's Word. The Eucharist, while commemorating the passion and resurrection, is also in continuity with the incarnation.

At the Annunciation Mary conceived the Son of God in the physical reality of His body and blood, thus anticipating within herself what to some degree happens sacramentally in every believer who receives, under the signs of bread and wine, the Lord's body and blood.

Let us listen to Mary Most Holy, in whom the mystery of the Eucharist appears, more than in anyone else, as a mystery of light. Gazing upon Mary, we come to know the transforming power present in the Eucharist.

In her we see the world renewed in love. Contemplating her, assumed body and soul into heaven, we see opening up before us those "new heavens" and that "new earth" which will appear at the second coming of Christ. Here below, the Eucharist represents their pledge, and in a certain way, their anticipation: *"Veni, Domine Iesu!"*

Pope John Paul II
***Ecclesia de Eucharistia*, 2003**

1.   *Come, Lord Jesus!* (Rev 22:20)

Henceforth all ages will call me blessed . (Lk 1:48)

PREPARATION FOR HOLY COMMUNION

O Most Blessed Virgin Mary, mother of gentleness and mercy, I, a miserable and unworthy sinner, fly to thy protection with every sentiment of humility and love; and I implore of thy loving kindness that thou wouldst graciously be near me, and all who throughout the whole Church are to receive the Body and Blood of thy Son this day, even as thou were near thy sweetest Son as He hung bleeding on the Cross, that, aided by thy gracious help, we may worthily offer up a pure and acceptable sacrifice in the sight of the Holy and Undivided Trinity.

Amen.

AFTER HOLY COMMUNION

O Most Holy, O good, noble and glorious Virgin Mary, who was worthy to bear in thy sacred womb the Creator of all, and at thy virginal breast to nourish Him Whose true, real, and most holy Body and Blood I, an unworthy sinner, have just now dared to receive; I humbly beseech thee to intercede with Him for me a sinner; that whatsoever, by ignorance or neglect, by accident or irreverence, I have left undone, or have done amiss, in this unspeakably holy Sacrifice, may be pardoned through thy prayers to the same Lord Jesus Christ, thy Son, Who with the Father and the Holy Ghost liveth and reigneth world without end.

Amen.

Ancient Devotions for Holy Communion

The Almighty works marvels for me. (Lk 1:49)

CHRIST-BEARER

The first *Corpus Christi* procession occurred in a certain sense when Mary, bearing the newly conceived Jesus in her womb, left Nazareth to visit her cousin Elizabeth. In contemplating this Gospel icon, may the Church hasten her steps towards contemporary man and proclaim to him with renewed love the Good News of salvation.

Pope John Paul II
Angelus Address, **Rome, June 1998**

There is a profound analogy between the *Fiat* which Mary said in reply to the angel, and the *Amen* which every believer says when receiving the body of the Lord. Mary was asked to believe that the One whom she conceived *"through the Holy Spirit"* was *"the Son of God"* (Lk 1:30-35). In continuity with the Virgin's faith, in the Eucharistic mystery we are asked to believe that the same Jesus Christ, Son of God and Son of Mary, becomes present in His full humanity and divinity under the signs of bread and wine.

"Blessed is she who believed" (Lk 1:45). Mary also anticipated, in the mystery of the incarnation, the Church's Eucharistic faith. When, at the Visitation, she bore in her womb the Word made flesh, she became in some way a "tabernacle" - the first "tabernacle" in history - in which the Son of God, still invisible to our human gaze, allowed Himself to be adored by Elizabeth, radiating His light as it were through the eyes and the voice of Mary. And is not the enraptured gaze of Mary as she contemplated the face of the newborn Christ and cradled Him in her arms that unparalleled model of love which should inspire us every time we receive Eucharistic communion?

Pope John Paul II
Ecclesia de Eucharistia, **2003**

MOTHER OF GOD

What dignity can be too great to attribute to her who is as closely bound up, as intimately one, with the Eternal Word, as a mother is with a son? Is it surprising then that on the one hand she should be immaculate in her conception? Or on the other that she should be honoured with an assumption, and exalted as a queen? Men sometimes wonder that we call her Mother of life, of mercy, of salvation; what are all these titles compared to that one name, Mother of God?

John Henry Cardinal Newman
Certain Difficulties felt by Anglicans in Catholic Teaching

Holy the womb that bore Him,
Holy the breasts that fed,
But holier still the royal heart
That in His passion bled.

John Henry Cardinal Newman
Meditations and Devotions

MOTHER OF THE CHURCH

Mary is present, with the Church and as the Mother of the Church, at each of our celebrations of the Eucharist. If the Church and the Eucharist are inseparably united, the same ought to be said of Mary and the Eucharist. This is one reason why, since ancient times, the commemoration of Mary has always been part of the Eucharistic celebrations of the Churches of East and West.

Pope John Paul II
Ecclesia de Eucharistia, **2003**

Holy His Name! (Lk 1:49)

THREE PRAYERS TO OUR LADY BEFORE COMMUNION

O most chaste Virgin Mary, I beseech thee by that unspotted purity wherewith thou didst prepare for the Son of God a dwelling of delights in thy virginal womb, that by thine intercession I may be cleansed from every stain.

O most humble Virgin Mary, I beseech thee by that most profound humility wherewith thou didst merit to be raised high above all the choirs of Angels and Saints, that by thine intercession all my negligences may be expiated.

O most amiable Virgin Mary, I beseech thee by that ineffable love which united thee so closely and inseparably to God, that by thine intercession I may obtain an abundance of all merit. Amen.

O Mary, our Hope, have pity upon us.

Taught by Our Lady to St Gertrude
(Approved by Pope Pius X)

PRAYER TO OUR LADY

No tongue or knowledge can have confidence,
Lady, to tell thy great humility,
Thy bounty, virtue and magnificence,
For sometimes, Lady, ere men pray to thee
Thou goest before them in benignity
And through thy prayer thou gettest for each one
Light that may guide them to thy blessed Son.

Geoffrey Chaucer
Fourteenth Century

MODEL FOR OUR PRAYER

What must Mary have felt as she heard from the mouth of Peter, John, James and the other Apostles the words spoken at the Last Supper: *"This is My body which is given for you"* (Lk 22:19)? The body given up for us and made present under sacramental signs was the same body which she had conceived in her womb! For Mary, receiving the Eucharist must have somehow meant welcoming once more into her womb that heart which had beat in unison with hers and reliving what she had experienced at the foot of the Cross.

Pope John Paul II
Ecclesia de Eucharistia, **2003**

Having received Jesus and enthroned Him in your hearts, remain quiet for a moment, not praying in words, but resting in silent adoration. When this moment is past, begin your thanksgiving, for which you may use with profit the four ends of the Holy Sacrifice - ADORATION, THANKSGIVING, SORROW, SUPPLICATION. The best model for our thanksgiving is Mary receiving the Lord in her womb.

St Peter Julian Eymard
Holy Communion

Virgin Mother of God,
He Whom the world cannot hold,
enclosed Himself in thy womb,
being made man.

Alleluia!

Gradual Verse
The Visitation of Our Blessed Lady
Roman Missal

Pray for us sinners. (Hail Mary)

PRAYER TO OUR LADY AFTER COMMUNION

O spotless Blessed Virgin, behold I possess Him
Whom thou didst conceive without sin,
Who in infancy did rest on thy motherly breasts,
Who when taken down from the Cross, was placed in thine
arms, Whom thou also didst receive most worthily
in this Most Holy Sacrament of the Altar!

I pray thee, O glorious Virgin Mary,
through all the proofs of love
which thy Son bestowed upon thee,
to obtain for me the grace also
generously to manifest my love for Him.

Obtain for me that my soul, like thine,
may be a handmaid of the Lord;
help me to return fitting thanks
for the great favour He has now bestowed upon me,
and pray for me that He may purify my heart and my body
from every stain of sin and make them His dwelling,
and constantly remain with me by His grace,
that all my conduct, my whole life
may be to His honour and my salvation.

Amen.

Anon

Mary the Dawn, Christ the perfect Day;
Mary the Gate, Christ the heavenly Way.
Mary the Root, Christ the mystic Vine;
Mary the Grape, Christ the sacred Wine.

Mary the Wheat-sheaf, Christ the living Bread;
Mary the Rose tree, Christ the Rose blood-red.
Mary the Font, Christ the cleansing Flood;
Mary the Chalice, Christ the saving Blood.

Mary the Temple, Christ the temple's Lord;
Mary the Shrine, Christ the God adored.
Mary the Beacon, Christ the Haven's Rest;
Mary the Mirror, Christ the Vision blest.

Medieval Hymn

Hail, Holy Queen, Mother of Mercy. (Salve Regina)

TO MARY OUR LADY

Mould of Christ's manhood
and chalice of His Blood,
Mary,
mother of us,
form us within you,
give us your spirit to drink.

Most fruitful of fields
where sprang the vine and grew the wheat,
Mary,
mother of us,
plant us in you
that we may grow into Christ.

Provident Mother of the Bread of Life,
spread your board
for the hungry of the world.

Mary, Ark of the Covenant,
the new and everlasting Covenant
in the Blood of Christ,
renew in us
fidelity to Christ
and to His covenant of love.

Brian Moore SJ
Prayers for Holy Communion

THE MAGNIFICAT

My soul glorifies the Lord,
my spirit rejoices in God, my Saviour.
He looks on His servant in her lowliness;
henceforth all ages will call me blessed.

The Almighty works marvels for me.
Holy His Name!
His mercy is from age to age,
on those who fear Him.

He puts forth His arm in strength
and scatters the proud-hearted.
He casts the mighty from their thrones
and raises the lowly.

He fills the starving with good things,
sends the rich away empty.

He protects Israel, His servant,
remembering His mercy,
the mercy promised to our fathers,
to Abraham and His sons forever.

(Lk1:46-55)

*Our Lady of the Most
Blessed Sacrament,
Pray for us.*

8

Priesthood and Consecrated Life

Pray the Lord of the harvest to send out labourers into His harvest

(Mt 9:38)

THE PRIEST
conscious of the full meaning of his priesthood, is the one

*who believes profoundly,
who professes his faith with courage,
who prays fervently,
who teaches with deep conviction,
who serves,
who puts into practice in his own life
the program of the beatitudes,
who knows how to love disinterestedly,
who is close to everyone,
especially to those who are most in need.*

Pope John Paul II
***Holy Thursday Letter to Priests**,* **Rome, April 1979**

Follow Me, and I will make you fishers of men. (Mt 4:19)

PRAYER FOR A PRIEST

O Jesus, Eternal Priest,
keep this Your servant within the shelter of Your
Sacred Heart, where none may harm him.
Keep unstained his anointed hands, which daily touch Your
Sacred Body.
Keep unsullied the lips purpled with
Your Precious Blood.
Keep pure and unearthly the heart sealed with the sublime mark
of Your glorious Priesthood.
Let Your holy love surround him and shield him from the
world's contagion.

Bless his labours with abundant fruit,
and may the souls to whom he ministers be here below his joy
and consolation
and in heaven his beautiful and everlasting crown.

Amen.

Anon

THE PRIEST AND THE EUCHARIST

I have always started my day with the celebration of the Eucharist, the pivot and heart of every priestly life, discovering each time with immense gratitude that it is the mysterious and essential bond which ties every priest to Christ the Redeemer. At the school of Jesus, Priest and Victim, I came increasingly to understand that the priest does not live for himself, but for the Church and for the sanctification of the People of God.

Pope John Paul II
speaking about the 50th anniversary
of his priestly ordination

THE PRIEST AND PRAYER

Never doubt that the Spirit, the Paraclete, will be your counsel and advocate and will give you the strength to overcome all obstacles. Continue therefore confident and secure in His power and may you experience relief and rest in frequent and prolonged prayer. Prayer unifies the priest's life which so often risks being fragmented by the multiplicity of the tasks he must undertake; prayer makes what you do authentic, because it draws from the Heart of Christ the sentiments that motivate your work. Do not be afraid to dedicate time and energy to it, indeed strive to be men of diligent prayer, enjoying the silence of contemplation and the devout daily celebration of the Eucharist and the Liturgy of the Hours which the Church has entrusted to you for the good of Christ's entire Body. The priest's prayer is also a requirement of his pastoral ministry, since Christian communities are enriched by the witness of the prayerful priest who proclaims the mystery of God with his words and with his life.

Pope John Paul II
Third International Meeting of Priests
Mexico, 1998

I shall offer within His tent a sacrifice of joy. (Ps 26:6)

THE PRIEST'S PRAYER - A SPIRIT OF SACRIFICE

Lord Jesus, You knew that mankind could only be saved by sacrifice, and You made Your whole life on earth a perpetual immolation.

Identified with You, acting as priest with You, when I celebrate Mass, O my Crucified God, I desire to be a victim with You. Everything in You revolves around Your Cross. Everything in me has to revolve around my Mass. It will be the centre, the sun of my days, just as Your Sacrifice is the central act of the Liturgy.

And the Liturgy will become, to me, a school of the spirit of sacrifice, because the altar and the Tabernacle will ever be taking me back to Calvary. By making me share in the thoughts and aspirations of Your Church, the Liturgy will communicate Your own sentiments to me, O Jesus, and thus will the words of St Paul be fulfilled in me: *"Let this mind be in you which was also in Christ Jesus,"* along with those other words that were spoken to me at my ordination: *Imitamini quod tractatis*[1].

Dom Chautard
The Soul of the Apostolate

1. Imitate what you perform.

UNFURL YOUR SAILS TO THE BREATH OF THE SPIRIT!

The Spirit is like a wind filling the sails of the great ship of the Church. If, however, we look at her closely, she uses numerous other small sails that are the hearts of the baptized. Everyone, dear friends, is invited to hoist his sail and unfurl it with courage, to permit the Spirit to act with all His sanctifying power. By allowing the Spirit to act in one's own life, one also makes the best contribution to the Church's mission.

Do not be afraid, dear seminarians, to unfurl your sails to the breath of the Spirit! Let His power of truth and love enliven every aspect of your existence: your spiritual commitment, the inmost intentions of your conscience, the deepening of your theological study and your experiences of pastoral service, your sentiments and affections, your very corporality.

Your whole being is called to respond to the Father through the Son in the Spirit, so that your whole person may become a sign and instrument of Christ, the Good Shepherd.

Pope John Paul II
Archdiocesan Seminary
Florence, April 1998

If the Church is lacking in priests, Jesus is lacking.
A community poor in vocations impoverishes the Church.
A community rich in vocations enriches the whole Church.

Pope John Paul II
Melbourne
November 1986

Come, follow Me. (Mt 19:21)

PRAYER FOR VOCATIONS

Lord Jesus Christ, You commanded us to pray for vocations. Call, we beseech You, many in our diocese to leave all things and follow You, for the glory of Your name and the salvation of souls. Amen.

Mary, Queen of Apostles, pray for us; obtain for us many holy priests and religious.

Heavenly Father, in Your loving design for all people, You sent Your only Son to earth to die on the cross for the salvation of every man and woman.

During His life on earth, Your Divine Son gathered to Himself disciples who were sent out to bring the Good News to all men and women.

We pray that You will touch the hearts of young men and women to follow You and so continue the salvation of the world.

Finally, give us the grace and courage to be faithful to our commitment.

We make this prayer through Christ, our Lord.

Amen.

Anon

THE PRIESTHOOD

The priesthood is the love of the Heart of Jesus. When you see the priest, think of Our Lord Jesus Christ.

St John Vianney
Catechism on the Priesthood

The heart of Jesus is in the priest. In choosing a man to be a priest, Jesus has given Himself totally to that man. It is only the priest who can give the real living Jesus to us - in the Blessed Sacrament. How pure the hearts of priests must be to be able to say: "This is My Body". How pure their hands must be to grant absolution at any time! It is very important that priests help the people to come close to Jesus. They need to help the people to have clean hearts, because a clean heart is able to see Christ.

Mother Teresa
Loving Jesus

DAILY EUCHARIST

How important it is for the spiritual life of the priest, as well as for the good of the Church and the world, that priests follow the (Second Vatican) Council's recommendation to celebrate the Eucharist daily: *"for even if the faithful are unable to be present, it is an act of Christ and the Church".*[1] In this way priests will be able to counteract the daily tensions which lead to a lack of focus and they will find in the Eucharistic Sacrifice – the true centre of their lives and ministry – the spiritual strength needed to deal with their different pastoral responsibilities. Their daily activity will thus become truly Eucharistic.

Pope John Paul II
Ecclesia de Eucharistia, 2003

1. *Presbyterorum Ordinis.*

*Put out into the deep
and let down your nets for a catch.* (Lk 5:4)

PRAYER FOR HOLY PRIESTS

O almighty and eternal God, look upon the face of Your Christ, and for the love of Him who is the eternal High Priest, have pity on Your priests. Remember, most compassionate God, that they are but weak and frail human beings. Stir up in them the grace of their vocation, which is in them by the laying-on of the Bishop's hands. Keep them close to You, lest the enemy prevail against them, so that they may never do anything in the slightest degree unworthy of their sublime vocation.

O Jesus, I pray to You for Your faithful and fervent priests; for Your unfaithful and lukewarm priests; for Your priests working hard at home or overseas in distant mission fields; for Your tempted priests; for Your lonely and desolate priests; for Your young priests; for Your aged priests; for Your sick priests; for Your dying priests; for the souls of Your priests in purgatory.

But above all, I commend to You the priests dearest to me: the priest who baptised me; the priests who absolved me from my sins; the priests at whose Masses I assisted and who have given me Your Body and Blood in Holy Communion; the priests who taught and instructed me or helped me or encouraged me; all the priests to whom I am indebted in any other way, particularly ...

O Jesus, keep them close to Your Heart, and bless them abundantly in time and in eternity.

Amen.

Fr. Bruno M. Hagspiel SVD

MASS - THE CENTRE OF PRIESTLY LIFE

On June 14, 1998, the Holy Father celebrated Mass with the community of the Roman Major Seminary. His homily, abridged, follows:

The Eucharistic sacrifice is the source and summit of the Church's life and of our personal journey of sanctification. (cf. *Lumen gentium,* n.11)

Mary Shows You the Altar

The Blessed Virgin, the Mother of priests, wants to lead all men to Christ; she knows that to do this she needs generous service from the holy ministers of the Eucharist. This is why Mary shows you the altar, which, from the day of a priest's ordination, is where his daily meeting with the Lord culminates. In fact, it is primarily at Holy Mass that the priest makes progress in his conformity to Christ.

"I have been crucified with Christ; it is no longer I who live, but Christ Who lives in me" (Gal 2:20). Paul's words to the Galatians are a synthesis of the existential fruit of Eucharistic communion: the indwelling of Christ in the soul, brought about by the Holy Spirit.

Who, more than the priest, is called to make these words his own and to offer them as a plan of life? Who, more than he, lives wholly on the Bread of eternal life, given by Christ for the world's salvation?

Passionately Love the Eucharist

Mass is truly the centre of the priest's life, the centre of all his days. This centrality is thus the primary objective of the seminary's formation programme, which requires the conscious and total co-operation of each candidate for the priesthood. First of all, the seminarian should passionately love the Eucharist: he should recognise that his vocation directs him towards a fervent and ever deeper participation in the Sacrifice of the Mass, a participation which at a certain point acquires the meaning of a most personal call.

The words "do this in memory of Me" speak to his heart with profound eloquence. He recognises the Eucharist as the living sacrament of Christ's grace and so feels he has nothing to offer in exchange but himself.

When this response of faith and love matures in a young man, the Church's heart rejoices; the heart of Mary rejoices, as her motherly concern anticipates and accompanies the flowering of every individual vocation.

I pray that you may become holy priests.

Just as the Holy Spirit moulded the priestly heart of Christ from Mary's womb to the ultimate sacrifice on the Cross and to the fullness of life of the Resurrection, may He form your hearts for the salvation of souls and the glory of God with the full maturity of Christ the Good Shepherd.

Amen!

Pope John Paul II
Rome, June 1998

CARE FOR THE 'SEED' OF YOUR VOCATION

The Holy Father spoke to the Roman Seminarian community in June, 1997. The following is an abridged text of his homily.

> *"The kingdom of God is as if a man should scatter seed upon the ground".* (Mk 4:26)

The name seminary refers to these words of Christ. The Latin word *seminarium* comes from *semen,* seed. Jesus says that the seed scattered upon the ground will sprout and grow whether man watches or sleeps: it sprouts and grows by night and day. "The earth produces of itself, first the blade, then the ear, then the full grain in the ear". (Mk 4:28)

The analogy with the priestly vocation is self-evident. It is like God's seed, scattered in human souls, which grows with its own force. But the seed, in order to grow, must be cared for. It is man who must sow, and it is man again who must watch over the seed's growth. It is necessary to prevent harmful forces, evil persons or natural disasters from destroying the tender shoots that are growing. And when they have reached maturity, man must put his hand to the sickle, as Christ says, because the field is ready for the harvest. (cf. Mk 4:29)

On another occasion Jesus observes:-

> *"The harvest is plentiful, but the labourers are few; pray therefore the Lord of the harvest to send out labourers into His harvest".* (Mt 9:37-38)

These words also refer to the seminary, the place where labourers are trained for the great harvest of God's kingdom, which extends to all countries and continents.

Pope John Paul II
Rome, June 1997

We belong to Him. (Ps 99:3)

INVOCATIONS

O Lord, give Your Church saintly priests and fervent religious.

O Mary, Queen of the clergy,
pray for us;
obtain for us many and holy priests.

HEART OF JESUS, SOURCE OF LIFE AND HOLINESS

The vitality of your religious family depends precisely on the intensity of your spiritual life, expressed primarily in prayer. The Heart of Jesus, dear friends, is the focal point of your consecration. That Jesus, on Whom the whole Church fixes her gaze shows contemporary man His Heart, the source of life and holiness. King and centre of all hearts, Christ asks consecrated persons not only to contemplate Him, but to enter into His Heart, to be able to live and work in constant communion with His sentiments.

Pope John Paul II
to *Priests of the Sacred Heart of Jesus*
Rome, 1997

NEVER FORSAKE PERSONAL PRAYER

I encourage you never to forsake personal, daily and extended prayer, that you may become more and more like Christ, the Good Shepherd; for in Him is found the principal source of energy and our true rest (Mt 11:30). In this way you will be able to face joyfully the burden of *"the day and the heat"* (Mt 20:12) and will thus give the best testimony for promoting the priestly and religious vocations which are so greatly needed.

Pope John Paul II
Cuba, January 1998

As the Father has sent Me even so I send you. (Jn 20:21)

PRAYER FOR THE
SANCTIFICATION OF PRIESTS

Father,
you have appointed your Son Jesus Christ
eternal high priest.
Guide those he has chosen
to be ministers of word and sacrament
and help them to be faithful
in fulfilling the ministry they have received.
Grant this through our Lord Jesus Christ, your Son,
who lives and reigns with you and the Holy Spirit,
one God, for ever and ever.

Mass for Priests
Opening Prayer
The Roman Missal

THE PRIEST
LIVING ICON OF THE GOOD SHEPHERD

On Good Shepherd Sunday, World Day of Prayer for Vocations, 25 April, 1999, the Holy Father ordained three new priests. An extract from his homily follows:

The Eucharist, the source and summit of the Christian life, will be the crystal clear spring that will constantly replenish your priestly spirituality. You will be able to draw from it the inspiration for your daily ministry, apostolic zeal for the work of evangelization and spiritual consolation in the inevitable moments of difficulty and inner struggle. By standing at the altar where the sacrifice of the Cross is renewed, you will increasingly discover the wealth of Christ's love and learn to express it in your life.

A vocation is rooted in the depths of conscience and of human freedom. It starts with a dialogue of love, which day after day moulds the priest's personality through a formation process begun in the family, continued in the seminary and extended throughout his life. Only through this uninterrupted ascetical and pastoral journey can the priest become a living icon of Jesus, the Good Shepherd, Who gives Himself for the flock entrusted to His care.

Imitate the mystery you celebrate. This mystery you dispense is really Christ Himself, who through the communication of the Holy Spirit is the source of holiness and a ceaseless call to sanctification. Imitate this mystery: imitate Christ, be Christ! May each of you be able to say with St Paul: *"It is no longer I who live, but Christ who lives in me".* (Gal 2:20).

Pope John Paul II
Rome, April 1999

Father, sanctify them in the truth...
As Thou didst send Me into the world, so
I have sent them into the world. (Jn 17:17-18)

PRAYER FOR PRIESTLY VOCATIONS

Father,
in your plan for salvation
you provide shepherds for your people.
Fill your Church with the spirit of courage and love.
Raise up worthy ministers for your altars
and ardent but gentle servants of the gospel.

Grant this through our Lord Jesus Christ, your Son,
who lives and reigns with you and the Holy Spirit,
one God, for ever and ever.

Mass for Priestly Vocations
Opening Prayer
The Roman Missal

ANOTHER CHRIST

A priest, clad in his sacred vestments, standeth in Christ's stead, to pray to God for himself and for all the people, in a suppliant and humble manner.

He hath before him and behind him the sign of the Lord's cross, that he may always remember the passion of Christ.

He beareth the cross before him on his vestment, that he may diligently behold the footsteps of Christ, and fervently endeavour to follow them.

He is marked with a cross behind, that he may meekly suffer, for God's sake, whatever adversities from others befall him.

He weareth the cross before him that he may bewail his own sins; and behind him that through compassion he may lament the sins of others, and know that he is placed as a mediator betwixt God and the sinner.

Neither ought he to cease from prayer and the holy oblation, till he be favoured with the grace and mercy which he implores.

When a priest celebrates Mass he honours God, rejoices the angels, edifies the Church, helps the living, obtains rest for the dead, and makes himself partaker of all good things.

Thomas à Kempis
The Imitation of Christ **(IV 5:3)**

It is no longer I who live but Christ Who lives in me. (Gal 2:20)

THE PRIEST AND THE MASS

My purpose is to celebrate Mass and to consecrate the Body and Blood of our Lord Jesus Christ according to the rite of the holy Roman Church, to the praise of almighty God and of the whole Church triumphant in heaven, for my own welfare and that of the whole Church militant on earth, for all who in general and in particular have commended themselves to my prayers, and for the well-being of the holy Roman Church.

May joy and peace, amendment of life, room for true penitence, the grace and comfort of the Holy Spirit, and steadfastness in good works be granted us by the almighty and merciful Lord.

Amen.

Priest's Declaration of purpose before Mass
The Roman Missal

The Blessed Eucharist is Your very self, O Jesus, under the appearance of bread. And each Mass makes it more clear to my eyes that the priest is Yourself, O sole Priest, under the appearance of a man, whom You have chosen for Your minister.

Dom Chautard
The Soul of the Apostolate

THE POWER OF THE PRIEST COMES FROM GOD HIMSELF

High is this ministry, and great the dignity of priests to whom that is given which is not granted to angels. For priests alone, rightly ordained in the Church, have power to celebrate and to consecrate the Body of Christ.

The priest, indeed, is the minister of God, using the word of God, and by the command and institution of God: but God Himself is there, the principal Author and invisible Worker, to Whom is subject whatever He willeth, and Whose command everything obeyeth.

Thomas à Kempis
The Imitation of Christ **(IV 5:1)**

PRIESTLY CHARITY INSPIRES VOCATIONS

The centrality of the Eucharist in the life and ministry of priests is the basis of its centrality in the pastoral promotion of priestly vocations. It is in the Eucharist that prayer for vocations is most closely united to the prayer of Christ the Eternal High Priest.

At the same time the diligence of priests in carrying out their Eucharistic ministry, together with the conscious, active and fruitful participation of the faithful in the Eucharist, provides young men with a powerful example and incentive for responding generously to God's call.

Often it is the example of a priest's fervent pastoral charity which the Lord uses to sow and to bring to fruition in a young man's heart the seed of a priestly calling.

Pope John Paul II
Ecclesia de Eucharistia, **2003**

You shall be holy. (Lev 19:2)

THE DIGNITY OF THE PRIESTHOOD

Oh! how great and honourable is the office of priests, to whom it is given to consecrate with sacred words the Lord of Majesty; to bless Him with their lips, to hold Him in their hands, to receive Him with their own mouth, and to administer Him to others!

Oh! how clean ought those hands to be, how pure that mouth, how holy that body, how unspotted the heart of a priest, into whom the Author of Purity so often entereth!

From the mouth of a priest nothing but what is holy, no word but what is good and profitable ought to proceed, who so often receiveth the sacrament of Christ.

Simple and chaste be the eyes, which are wont to behold the Body of Christ; pure and lifted up to heaven the hands, which are used to handle the Creator of heaven and earth.

Unto priests especially it is said in the law, *Be you holy, for I the Lord your God am holy.* (Lev 19:2)

Thomas à Kempis
The Imitation of Christ **(IV 11:6-7)**

"BE HOLINESS" IN THE HEART OF THE CHURCH

The witness of consecrated persons makes tangible in the midst of God's People the spirit of the Beatitudes, the value of the great commandment of love of God and love of neighbour. In a word, consecrated persons are at the very heart of the mystery of the Church, the Bride who responds to Christ's infinite love with her whole being. How could we Bishops fail to praise God unceasingly and be filled with gratitude for such a gift to His Church!

In our day, as throughout the history of the Church, consecrated women and men stand out as living icons of what it means to make the following of Jesus the whole purpose of one's life and to be transformed by His grace. I appeal to all consecrated persons, and to the men and women who may be thinking of entering a community, to renew each day their awareness of the extraordinary privilege that is theirs: the call to serve the holiness of God's People, to "be holiness" in the heart of the Church.

Pope John Paul II
to US Bishops in Rome, 1998

THE RESPONSIBILITY OF PRIESTS

A great responsibility belongs to priests in particular for the celebration of the Eucharist. It is their responsibility to preside at the Eucharist *in persona Christi* and to provide a witness to and a service of communion not only for the community directly taking part in the celebration, but also for the universal Church, which is a part of every Eucharist. Priests who faithfully celebrate Mass according to the liturgical norms, and communities which conform to those norms, quietly but eloquently demonstrate their love for the Church.

Pope John Paul II
Ecclesia de Eucharistia, 2003

If you would be perfect, go, sell what you possess, and give to the poor and come, follow Me. (Mt 19:21)

PRAYER FOR RELIGIOUS VOCATIONS

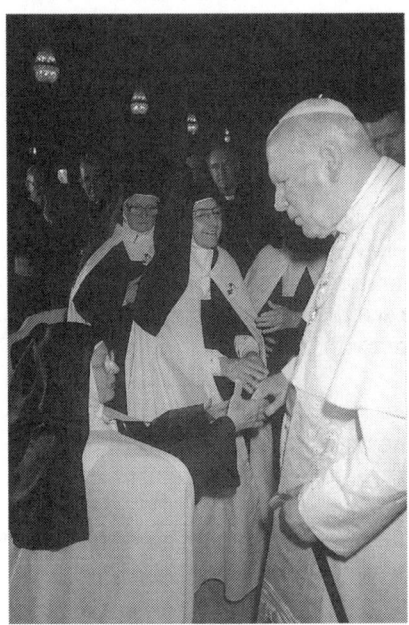

Father,
in your love accept the gifts we offer you,
and watch over those who wish to follow your Son more closely,
and to serve you joyfully in religious life.
Give them spiritual freedom
and love for their brothers and sisters.

We ask this through Christ our Lord.

Mass for Religious Vocations
Prayer over the gifts
The Roman Missal

HOLY FATHER'S PRAYER FOR PRIESTLY VOCATIONS

Good Father,
in Christ Your Son You reveal to us Your love,
You embrace us as Your children
and You offer us the possibility
of discovering in Your will the lines of our true face.

Holy Father,
You call us to be holy as You are holy.
We pray You, never allow Your Church
to lack holy ministers and apostles who,
with the word and the sacraments, may open the way
to the encounter with You.

Merciful Father,
give to lost humanity men and women who,
through the witness of a life transfigured
to the image of Your Son,
may walk joyfully with their other brothers and sisters
towards our heavenly homeland.

Our Father,
with the voice of Your Holy Spirit,
and trusting in the maternal intercession of Mary,
we earnestly beseech You:
send to Your Church priests
who will be courageous witnesses
to Your infinite bounty.

Amen!

Pope John Paul II
36th World Day of Prayer for Vocations, **Rome, April 1999**

9

Prayers of the People

Lord, teach us to pray

(Lk 11:22)

In places of perpetual adoration, many people write their petitions in an intention book provided so that others, too, may pray for them. Some of these prayers, selected from perpetual adoration parishes across Australia, are included here.

They are an eloquent testimony to the love, unity and prayerfulness which overflow in communities where the focal point of parish life is the Blessed Eucharist, Christ's presence during the Mass and abiding afterwards.

OFFERING

O my God, You are so good! I offer You all the love and adoration of all those who come here to pray in union with all the Masses offered in our Church.

Dearest Jesus, I offer You my exhaustion tonight in reparation for my sins and those of all who offend You. I offer You all the prayers of your friends who come to adore You perpetually here in our parish for all the intentions of Your Sacred Heart.

O Jesus, I offer my adoration, praise and love to make up for abortion, war and evil. I offer my Holy Hour for the dying and the Holy Souls.

I offer You my Holy Hour, dear Lord, in union with the hours of all the adorers in our parish, of those whose daily work involves sweat and toil and those who labour with their minds. May we glorify You in our word and our prayer and appreciate ever more fully Your living Presence among us.

Dear Jesus, my Jesus, I offer You my nothingness and You give me Your forgiveness. Help me to do likewise to all I meet.

FOR FAMILIES

Dear Jesus, You have blessed this small and beautiful Chapel so that we can come to pray for our families, our society and all the world. I am grateful for Your love and the well-being of my family. Please let my prayers be heard for those who do not yet know Your love, for the old, especially those who are lonely and sick and for mothers who are often exhausted.

Dear Jesus, I give You thanks and praise for all the gifts You have given me and my family. Help us always to persevere in our faith and be with us always.

Dear Jesus, thank You for the opportunity of being with You for this time as I pray for the members of my family ... bring them close to You and give them a greater understanding of their faith. Dear Lord I pray that You will soften my concrete heart and open my life to Your love. Dear Lord please help all the young people all over the world and ask Your dear mother Mary to guide them.

FOR PRIESTS

Lord Jesus, thank You for the gift of Your presence and the privilege of this Hour. I offer it for the sanctification of priests and the conversion of sinners.

Blessed Saviour, I offer this Holy Hour for all the intentions of our Holy Father and for an increase in vocations, especially to the priesthood and religious life.

Dearest Jesus, thank You for the many graces You have showered on our parish priest. Please continue to inspire him. Increase his holiness, his courage and his wisdom. Thank You for this very rare good shepherd. May any suffering he has be given to me instead.

Dearest Jesus, we praise You and thank You for the wonderful blessings You have bestowed on our family by choosing our son to be a priest. Please guide and protect him during his time at the seminary.

THANKSGIVING

Dear Lord Jesus, thank You for being here. May more people come to know the joy of finding You in Your Eucharistic presence and may You be at the centre of our lives and our hearts. Help us all to grow deeply in Your love and to appreciate more and more how much You love us.

Heavenly Father, we give You thanks for Jesus in the Blessed Eucharist.

My dear Jesus, thank You for the great pleasure You give us in being here - always available. Thank You for the joy of knowing that You are loved much here.

Dear Lord, we thank You for opening this door for us. We pray that we may always keep the Holy Hour free so as to come to You with love and thanksgiving in our hearts. Lord, we ask You to use us so we may bring others to You and to our Heavenly Mother Mary.

Dear Jesus, thank You for Your Eucharistic love. Thank You for my family. Make us grow in love, in Your love. Draw us close to You. Thank You for priests. Bring them all close to Your Sacred Heart.

We thank You for every moment with You, Lord Jesus.

SPECIAL REQUESTS

Keep all those You have called to keep You company to persevere in this great undertaking, hour by hour, day by day. Help us to keep our eyes firmly on You, dear Lord, so that one day we will feast our eyes on You for all eternity, never to be separated from You again.

Dear Lord, I pray that other parishes may follow this perpetual adoration. May we be more aware of the precious gift of Your presence among us.

Dear Lord, teach me to listen to You when I can't pray. Help me to love You as I ought.

Dearest Lord, please guide our parish. Thank You for all the graces and the joys You give us. May the sorrows, too, bring us always closer to You. Unite us in Your love and bring us ever closer to Your heavenly Father.

NOCTURNAL ADORATION

I kneel before You, Lord
It is night: it is quiet.
My warm bed beckons: sleep calls.
Human folly indeed to deny
the body what it needs.
What madness is this?
But Your presence, Lord,
is stronger than this.
Your peace overcomes
all human weakness and pain,
A much greater call than
sleep or warmth.
Your Spirit is here, Lord,
A chance to love and pray.
Divine Wisdom: that's it!
It makes sense at last.
An hour with my Saviour, my God.
St Thomas was right -
'My Lord and my God'
How can this compare with
things of this world,
The peace You offer and share?
For me You died, Lord.
While the world sleeps,
To watch and pray,
To sink into the depths
of Your love, Lord,
To entrust to You all the needs
of Your people - my people-
And souls long departed.
There is greater warmth here, Lord,
than any bed, any home.
This is Your wisdom indeed.

Divine Wisdom

10

Perpetual Adoration

*I am with you always,
even to the end
of the world*

(Mt 28:20)

PERPETUAL ADORATION

Perpetual adoration is continuous prayer in the presence of Jesus in the tabernacle or monstrance. Successive adorers undertake to make a weekly holy hour of prayer once a week. These Holy Hours continue day and night without ceasing.

Adoration of the Blessed Sacrament has been practised since early Christian times. Devotion to the Holy Eucharist grew gradually over the centuries. By the thirteenth century, Northern European countries, especially Belgium, were marked by intense devotion to the Sacred Host involving reservation of the Blessed Sacrament in the tabernacle, displaying the Host in an ostensorium on the altar and ceremonies of Benediction. In 1246, the Bishop of Liège authorised a special feast day dedicated to *"the Body of the Lord."* (Corpus Domini)

There has been perpetual adoration in France at the Basilica of the Sacred Heart of Montmartre in Paris since 1885. In Australia perpetual adoration began in 1881, at the Convent of the Sisters of Perpetual Adoration in Brisbane. Shortly after his election in 1978, Pope John Paul II established perpetual adoration of the Blessed Sacrament in Rome. He has vigorously promoted Eucharistic Adoration throughout his pontificate.

In the United States there are approximately 1,100 parishes with perpetual adoration. In the Philippines there are about 500 perpetual adoration chapels. In the Republic of Ireland there are 150 and in South Korea there are 70.

In 1986, the Perpetual Eucharistic Adoration Association was founded by Owen Traynor, an Australian living in the United States. The Holy Father, Pope John Paul II, presented Owen Traynor with a monstrance and said:

"Thank you for this evangelical work promoting Eucharistic adoration. It is a grace for the Church. You have my encouragement and blessing."[1]

On this occasion Mother Teresa gave her whole-hearted support: *"Perpetual adoration is the most beautiful thing you could ever think of doing. People are hungry for God."*[2]

The Perpetual Eucharistic Adoration Association was given Pontifical approval in 1991. Perpetual adoration has grown rapidly, particularly in the US, the Philippines, Ireland, Mexico, Korea, Thailand, Canada and Puerto Rico.

Personal Prayer

Those who spend a regular weekly Holy Hour in the Eucharistic presence of Jesus claim that this hour each week has changed their lives. They have a secure place of peace and tranquillity where they can pray, apart from the hustle and bustle of daily life.

They develop an intimate friendship with Our Lord. They share their lives with Him, but He too shares His Divine Life with them. They tell Him their joys, their inner thoughts, their secrets, their problems. He, in turn, imparts His way of thinking, His way of living, of acting, His charm. They begin to take on His words, His actions, His thoughts. The Eucharistic Jesus becomes in a very real sense the centre of their Christian life and the source of their strength.

1. Reprinted from L'Osservatore Romano, English edition
2. Perpetual Eucharistic Adoration Newsletter, Vol.1, No.1 Easter 1987

Their problems do not evaporate, but they are given an added strength to cope with them. They are able to unite their crosses more fully with the Cross of Christ and their dignity takes on a divine dimension. They develop a greater appreciation of the Mass and the graces of Holy Communion and Confession.

Family Life

Perpetual adoration enhances family life. Those who pray regularly in the presence of Jesus in the Eucharist grow in openness to the workings of the Holy Spirit and thereby become more tolerant, more loving, more thoughtful. Families cannot but become happier, more united in this atmosphere.

Where Jesus is loved and reverenced, God is generous with His graces, granting security, happiness and intimacy in family life. He blesses apostolic endeavours, gives courage and endurance in trials, widens perception of His presence in the lives of others, strengthens charity and willingness to serve. His most treasured gift is that of vocations to the priesthood and religious life.

Parish Life

When parishes begin Eucharistic adoration, the fervour of the faithful increases markedly. This is exemplified in an increase in daily and Sunday Mass attendance, numbers spending time in adoration and thanksgiving before and after Mass, a deepening in community and personal prayer, an increase in devotion and reverence within the church, a heightened appreciation of the Sacraments, silence in the presence of the Blessed Eucharist, and parish unity.

Lay Participation

Eucharistic adoration is, first and foremost, a lay initiative. Individual lay people make personal contact, inviting others to make Holy Hours, following up with phone-calls and making friendly reminders. It is lay people who establish prayer rosters, slotting adorers into time-slots every hour of the day and night. It is lay people who beautify the sanctuary, do the cleaning and polishing, arrange the flowers, sew and care for the altar linen, sing and conduct the choirs that make music to glorify God at Mass and Benediction.

The Role of the Priest

Experience has shown that perpetual adoration is sustainable and successful where the priest supports the work of the laity. It is the priest who is the key factor in the success of perpetual adoration. It is not that he needs to spend time making the process work. He already has much to do in his parish. But if the priest lacks interest or is only half-committed, it is very difficult for perpetual adoration to succeed.

A perpetual adoration parish needs a priest who is entirely centred on the Holy Eucharist. Every one of his actions speaks volumes about his attitude to Christ in the Eucharist.

The priest can actively encourage perpetual adoration in many ways, by his example and silent witness as much as by his actions. The priest who places love for Jesus in the Eucharist at the heart of his own spiritual life demonstrates this by his demeanour during the celebration of Mass, his devotion outside of Mass and time spent in prayer and thanksgiving. These tangible signs of witness inspire the faithful, and Eucharistic love grows within the parish community.

The Eucharistic faith and practice of the faithful can be encouraged in an active way by the priest's regular preaching on the Eucharist, on prayer and adoration. His encouragement and gentle but firm insistence on silence in the presence of the Blessed Sacrament is a key factor in establishing and maintaining reverence in the church always.

If we desire parishes imbued with love for Jesus in the Eucharist, we need to pray for priests who are moulded in the image of the Good Shepherd. We expect our priests to be saints from the very day they are ordained but it takes a lifetime to achieve sanctity and holy priests need holy people to pray for them.

The Parish Community

Perpetual adoration rosters are not easy to maintain. Someone, or a number of people, should take charge of this. Prayer slots on adoration rosters are constantly becoming vacant due to illness, death, people moving great distances from the church, changes in family, work or study schedules, and even lack of interest. Hopefully, some adorers will leave to join seminaries and religious houses of formation.

If perpetual adoration is to flourish in a parish, the whole parish community has to accept ownership of its success. Every person on the roster has to be filled with a drive and enthusiasm that is sometimes proclaimed loudly, sometimes quietly, yet always powerfully. Constant invitations to join the prayer roster need to be personally extended to others. The most successful way to build up perpetual adoration in a parish is to invite individuals, one by one. It takes time, patience and a great deal of prayer and sacrifice.

The perpetual adoration parish has to be, first and foremost, apostolic. The ideal would be that every practising member of the parish would be making a weekly Holy Hour of prayer in the parish church. Every organised group in the parish should be represented on the roster of perpetual adoration: Legion of Mary, St Vincent de Paul, Bible study group, acolytes, readers, musicians, sacristans, catechists, teachers in the parish school, parents, children, the elderly.

Everyone should be warmly welcomed. Everyone should be given the opportunity to be a part of this Eucharistic apostolate, which is crucial to the spiritual life of individuals and the whole Church.

In some parishes, nocturnal hours of adoration are sustained by the men of the parish. This is the practice at the Basilica of the Sacred Heart in Paris when the doors close to the public at 6pm. Thereafter, the adoration continues, with the men of Paris praying all night. Some parishes have Children's Adoration groups, a practice which continues today in some parts of France, in particular at Paray-le-Monial.

If a parish is to be wholly centred on the Blessed Eucharist, there has to be a good deal of inspiration and mutual support within the parish community.

Many parishes have Prayer Intention Books near the sanctuary or in some other accessible place, so that prayer requests can be offered by others on the roster.

Parishes with readily accessible piety stalls can provide a wealth of material about adoration, how to make a Holy Hour, how to pray, and books on the saints, all of whom had a strong devotion to the Blessed Eucharist.

A properly functioning and well-maintained lending library of Eucharistic material, comprising books, pamphlets, videos and cassettes about the Holy Eucharist and about prayer can be of great assistance to parishioners and those on the adoration roster. This is an insurance against lack of enthusiasm when difficulties in prayer sometimes make it hard to maintain ardour and loyalty to one's Holy Hour.

Many people do not understand that growth in the spiritual life is often accompanied by difficulties in prayer. Assistance in this area can prevent spiritual stagnation and increase love and willingness to endure, even in hardship.

Some perpetual adoration parishes have established a Prayer Hot-Line, where adorers may phone in their prayer intentions or seek answers to their questions on prayer and growth in the spiritual life.

Prayer groups led by a competent person gifted in the practice and art of prayer can provide weekly direction. This form of direction can be invaluable and can teach adorers to use their Holy Hour effectively, whilst also providing knowledge and experience in the practice of different ways of praying.

Eucharistic Missions

Eucharistic faith and practice can be stimulated by organising parish Eucharistic Missions. The parish is visited for a weekend by a missionary priest. Homilies at all Masses and at other times throughout the weekend are aimed at building up Eucharistic faith and love within the parish community. Parishioners are invited to make a Holy Hour with Jesus exposed in the monstrance. Eucharistic adoration continues throughout the weekend.

Weekend Eucharistic Missions have proven to be a powerful stimulus to Eucharistic faith within the parish community. When people are given the opportunity to "taste and see the goodness of the Lord" in His Eucharistic presence, they want to spend time regularly in Eucharistic prayer. Many parishes have commenced Eucharistic adoration after experiencing a weekend Eucharistic Mission.

Eucharistic Retreats

Annual Eucharistic Retreats, to which every parishioner is invited, also serve to inspire love for Jesus in the Eucharist. Exposition continues throughout the Retreat and homilies on the Holy Eucharist are given between the Retreat Mass and Benediction, which closes the Retreat. There is an increased sense of unity in the parish when the faithful pray together in silence before the exposed Blessed Sacrament.

Eucharistic Processions

Public Eucharistic processions to celebrate the Feast of Corpus Christi and Christ the King are another way of inspiring the entire community to express Eucharistic faith and love. The Eucharistic procession can be short - conducted around the parish church - or it can be a public demonstration of faith - through the streets of the city.

At the beginning of his pontificate, Pope John Paul II re-introduced the public Eucharistic procession to Rome. Each year on the Feast of Corpus Christi, the Blessed Sacrament is carried in solemn procession from the Basilica of St John Lateran to the Basilica of St Mary Major, where Benediction is given on the steps overlooking the square. Thousands of people take part in this awe-inspiring devotion carrying lighted candles and singing beautiful Latin hymns to honour the Blessed Sacrament.

There are public Eucharistic processions in many parts of the world. These stimulate the faith of the people whilst providing an opportunity to come together in unity sharing Eucharistic belief and love.

Eucharistic Congresses

The Eucharistic Congress is another important stimulus to growth in Eucharistic faith. There have been national Eucharistic Congresses in major cities throughout the world since the first Congress was held in Lille, France, in 1881. International Eucharistic Congresses are usually conducted every two or three years.

The 47th International Eucharistic Congress, attended by 50 cardinals, 250 bishops, more than 1,000 priests and 100,000 faithful from around the world, was held in Rome in 2000. This was described by the Holy Father as *"the heart of the Great Jubilee of the Year 2000, an extraordinary expression of faith and an eloquent testimony of ecclesial communion."*

The week of Masses, catecheses, nocturnal adoration and apostolic camaraderie with Christians of like-mind contributed to an unforgettable week of grace and spiritual growth. It also provided invaluable stimulus to those who returned home inspired to promote Eucharistic adoration in their own parishes.

Perpetual Adoration in Australia

In 1881, the Sisters of Perpetual Adoration, a congregation founded by Father Julian Tennison Woods, began perpetual adoration in Brisbane, Australia.

In Warwick, Queensland, there was perpetual adoration at St Mary's parish from 1950 continuously for thirty-four years and thereafter for extended hours of adoration. The parish has been rich in vocations.

In Australia, perpetual Eucharistic adoration began in the 1980's in Western Australia. The devotion spread rapidly to Victoria and New South Wales.

In July 1993, the Society for Eucharistic Adoration was founded in Sydney. This lay organisation seeks to promote all forms of Eucharistic adoration and in particular perpetual adoration wherever this is possible. The only requirement for membership is to make a Holy Hour of prayer in the presence of the Blessed Sacrament once a week in any church or chapel, preferably in one's own parish, for this is a witness in one's own community.

Members of the Society for Eucharistic Adoration include members of the hierarchy, priests and religious, but principally lay people, in all states and territories in Australia and in the United Kingdom, United States, Italy, India, Solomon Islands, Malawi, Mauritius, Fiji, New Zealand and Thailand.

Perpetual Adoration and the Future

The latter two decades of the twentieth century have seen a movement towards Eucharistic devotion that is unique in the history of the Church. This is lay-inspired, lay-organised and lay-maintained adoration which promotes, directly and indirectly, personal holiness at its heart. It encourages a deepening of prayer life in the souls of lay people and inspires a love and intimacy with Jesus in His most profound presence we have on this earth, His Real Presence in the Most Holy Eucharist.

A quiet, gentle revolution is taking place in the Church, a renaissance of prayer, inspired by the Holy Spirit, reforming the lives of the faithful, pouring grace on individual souls and whole parishes across the world.

If we are to achieve true peace on this earth, peace in individual hearts and peace in whole nations, it is surely to be through prayer and through the most powerful prayer of all, in the presence of Jesus in the Eucharist.

Mother Teresa assured us of the importance of Eucharistic adoration in the lives of her sisters. The implications for all the faithful are obvious:

"In 1973, our congregation decided to have adoration for one hour every day. From that time, our love for Jesus became more intimate, our love for each other more compassionate, and we have doubled the number of vocations."

In 1993, Pope John Paul II made his fourth pastoral visit to Spain, where he attended the 45th International Eucharistic Congress. There, in Bologna, he made the following request:

"If only this form of (continuous) adoration, which ends tonight in a solemn Eucharistic vigil, would continue in the future too, so that in all the parishes and Christian communities the custom of some form of adoration of the Eucharist might take root."

Appendix of Prayers

THE HOLY ROSARY

| *Mysteries* | *Fruits of the Mysteries* |

JOYFUL MYSTERIES

1. The Annunciation	Humility
2. The Visitation	Charity
3. The Birth of Our Lord	Poverty, detachment from the world
4. The Presentation	Purity of heart, obedience
5. The Finding of the Child Jesus in the Temple	Piety

MYSTERIES OF LIGHT

1. Baptism of Our Lord in the Jordan	Openness to the Holy Spirit
2. The self-manifestation of Our Lord at the wedding of Cana	The faith of Mary
3. The proclamation of the Kingdom of God and the call to conversion	Solidarity with the poor
4. The Transfiguration of Our Lord	Fearlessness
5. The institution of the Eucharist	Unconditional love

SORROWFUL MYSTERIES

1. The Agony in the Garden — Sorrow for our sins

2. The Scourging at the Pillar — Mortification of our senses

3. The Crowning with Thorns — Disciplining the mind and soul

4. The Carrying of the Cross — Patience under crosses

5. The Crucifixion — Acceptance of God's will

GLORIOUS MYSTERIES

1. The Resurrection — Conversion of heart

2. The Ascension of Our Lord — The desire for Heaven

3. The Descent of the Holy Spirit on the Apostles and Our Lady. — The gifts of the Holy Spirit

4. The Assumption of Our Lady into Heaven — An increase in devotion to Our Lady

5. The Coronation of Our Lady — Eternal happiness

THE STATIONS OF THE CROSS

My Lord Jesus Christ, Thou hast made this journey to die for me with love unutterable, and I have so many times unworthily abandoned Thee; but now I love Thee with my whole heart, and because I love Thee, I repent sincerely for having ever offended Thee. Pardon me, my God, and permit me to accompany Thee on this journey. Thou goest to die for love of me; I wish also, my beloved Redeemer, to die for love of Thee. My Jesus, I will live and die always united to Thee.

BEFORE EVERY STATION

We adore Thee, O Christ and we praise Thee
because by Thy holy Cross Thou hast redeemed the world.

AFTER EVERY STATION

Our Father
Hail Mary
Glory be to the Father.
O Jesus, Who for love of me
didst bear Thy Cross to Calvary,
in Thy sweet mercy grant to me
to suffer and to die with Thee.

TRADITIONAL STATIONS OF THE CROSS

1. Jesus is condemned to die.

2. Jesus takes up His Cross.

3. Jesus falls the first time.

4. Jesus meets His sorrowful Mother.

5. Simon of Cyrene helps Jesus carry His Cross.

6. Veronica wipes the Face of Jesus.

7. Jesus falls the second time.

8. Jesus comforts the women of Jerusalem.

9. Jesus falls the third time.

10. Jesus is stripped of His garments.

11. Jesus is nailed to the Cross.

12. Jesus dies on the Cross.

13. Jesus is taken down from the Cross.

14. Jesus is laid in the tomb.

SCRIPTURAL STATIONS OF THE CROSS

On Good Friday, 1991, Pope John Paul II officiated at a Scriptural Way of the Cross in the Colosseum in Rome. The Stations were as follows:-

1. Jesus prays in the Garden of Gethsemane (Lk 22:39-46)

2. Jesus is betrayed by Judas (Mt 26:45-49)

3. Jesus is condemned by the Sanhedrin (Mk 14:56, 61-64)

4. Jesus is denied by Peter (Lk 22:54-62)

5. Jesus is condemned by the people (Lk 23:20-25)

6. Jesus is crowned with thorns and clothed in purple (Jn 19:1-3)

7. Jesus carries the cross (Jn 19:17)

8. Jesus is assisted by Simon of Cyrene (Mk 15:20-21)

9. Jesus meets the women of Jerusalem (Lk 23:27-31)

10. Jesus is crucified (Mk 15:22-26)

11. Jesus speaks to the thief (Lk 23:39-43)

12. Jesus speaks to His Mother (Jn 19:25-27)

13. Jesus dies on the cross (Mt 27:45-50)

14. Jesus is buried (Mt 27:57-61)

THE SEVEN LAST WORDS OF CHRIST ON THE CROSS

1. Father, forgive them, for they know not what they do.
   (Lk 23:34)

2. Truly, I say to you, today you will be with Me in Paradise.
   (Lk 23:43)

3. Woman, behold thy Son. Son, behold thy Mother.
   (Jn 19:26)

4. My God, my God, why hast Thou forsaken Me?
   (Mt 27:46)

5. I thirst.
   (Jn 19:28)

6. It is finished.
   (Jn 19:30)

7. Father, into Thy hands I commit My spirit.
   (Lk 23:46)

THE LITANY OF
THE MOST SACRED HEART OF JESUS

LORD, have mercy on us.
Christ, have mercy on us.
Lord, have mercy on us.
Christ, hear us.
Christ, graciously hear us.
God, the Father of Heaven,*
God the Son, Redeemer of the world,
God, the Holy Spirit,
Holy Trinity, One God,
Heart of Jesus, Son of the Eternal Father,
Heart of Jesus, formed by the Holy Spirit in the womb of the Virgin Mother,
Heart of Jesus, substantially united to the Word of God,
Heart of Jesus, of Infinite Majesty,
Heart of Jesus, Sacred Temple of God,
Heart of Jesus, Tabernacle of the Most High,
Heart of Jesus, House of God and Gate of Heaven,
Heart of Jesus, burning furnace of charity,
Heart of Jesus, abode of justice and love,
Heart of Jesus, full of goodness and love,
Heart of Jesus, abyss of all virtues,
Heart of Jesus, most worthy of all praise,
Heart of Jesus, King and centre of all hearts,
Heart of Jesus, in Whom are all the treasures of wisdom and knowledge,
Heart of Jesus, in Whom dwells the fullness of divinity,
Heart of Jesus, in Whom the Father was well pleased,
Heart of Jesus, of Whose fullness we have all received,
Heart of Jesus, desire of the everlasting hills,
Heart of Jesus, patient and most merciful,
Heart of Jesus, enriching all who invoke You,
Heart of Jesus, fountain of life and holiness,
Heart of Jesus, propitiation for our sins,*

* *Have mercy on us*

Heart of Jesus, loaded
  down with reproaches,
Heart of Jesus, bruised
  for our offences,
Heart of Jesus, obedient
  unto death,
Heart of Jesus, pierced with
  a lance.
Heart of Jesus, source of
  all consolation,
Heart of Jesus, our life
  and resurrection,
Heart of Jesus, our peace
  and reconciliation,
Heart of Jesus, Victim for
  our sins,
Heart of Jesus, salvation
  of those who trust in You,
Heart of Jesus, hope of
  those who die in You,
Heart of Jesus, delight
  of all the Saints,*
Lamb of God, You Who
take away the sins of the
world, *spare us, O Lord.*

Lamb of God, You Who
take away the sins of the
world, *graciously hear us,
O Lord.*

Lamb of God, You Who take
away the sins of the world,
have mercy on us.

V. Jesus, meek and
humble of heart.

R. Make our hearts like
  unto Yours.

* *Have mercy on us*

LET US PRAY

ALMIGHTY and eternal God, look upon the Heart of Your most beloved Son and upon the praises and satisfaction which He offers You in the name of sinners; and to those who implore Your mercy, of Your great goodness, grant forgiveness in the name of the same Jesus Christ, Your Son, Who with You lives and reigns in the unity of the Holy Spirit, God, world without end.

R. Amen.

DIVINE MERCY CHAPLET

Our Father ...

Hail Mary ...

I Believe in God ...

On the *Our Father* beads of the rosary:
"Eternal Father, I offer You the Body and Blood, Soul and Divinity of Your dearly beloved Son, Our Lord Jesus Christ, in atonement for our sins and those of the whole world."

On the *Hail Mary* beads:
"For the sake of His sorrowful Passion have mercy on us and on the whole world."

In conclusion, three times:
"Holy God, Holy Mighty One, Holy Immortal One, have mercy on us and on the whole world."

Prayer given to St Maria Faustina Kowalska in 1935

O MY GOD, TRINITY WHOM I ADORE

O my God, Trinity Whom I adore, help me to forget myself entirely that I may be established in You as still and as peaceful as if my soul were already in eternity. May nothing trouble my peace or make me leave You, O my Unchanging One, but may each minute carry me further into the depths of Your Mystery. Give peace to my soul; make it Your heaven, Your beloved dwelling and Your resting place. May I never leave You there alone but be wholly present, my faith wholly vigilant, wholly adoring, and wholly surrendered to Your creative Action.

O my beloved Christ, crucified by love, I wish to be a bride for Your Heart; I wish to cover You with glory; I wish to love You - even unto death! But I feel my weakness, and I ask You to "clothe me with Yourself," to identify my soul with all the movements of Your Soul, to overwhelm me, to possess me, to substitute Yourself for me that my life may be but a radiance of Your Life. Come into me as Adorer, as Restorer, as Saviour. O Eternal Word, Word of my God, I want to spend my life in listening to You, to become wholly teachable that I may learn all from You. Then, through all nights, all voids, all helplessness, I want to gaze on You always and remain in Your great light. O my beloved Star, so fascinate me that I may not withdraw from Your radiance.

O consuming Fire, Spirit of Love, "come upon me," and create in my soul a kind of incarnation of the Word: that I may be another humanity for Him in which He can renew His whole Mystery. And You, O Father, bend lovingly over Your poor little creature; "cover her with Your shadow," seeing in her only the "Beloved in whom You are well pleased."

O my Three, my All, my Beatitude, infinite Solitude, O Immensity in which I lose myself; I surrender myself to You as Your prey. Bury Yourself in me that I may bury myself in You until I depart to contemplate in Your light the abyss of Your greatness.

Blessed Elizabeth of the Trinity
November 21, 1904

THE ANGEL OF THE EUCHARIST
(from a play)

This angel comes forward ...

1. My brother angel, now see
   The Lord up to Heaven go!
   I am come down here, to be
   At the altar, bending low;
   Where now, to the sight of all,
   Almighty God, who is hid -
   Life's Author! - seems yet more small
   Than as new-born child He did.

Ref. Henceforth in this holy place -
   Ah, from here I will not move!
   My prayer to God I shall raise,
   Shall offer my hymns of love.

2. My lyre His Beauty recite,
   This hidden God! as I wait
   Caught up in holy delight,
   His charms that intoxicate.
   If only I, too, could feed
   On the God of Love each day! -
   By a miracle indeed,
   Unite with Him in that way.

Ref. Oh, at least to souls in grace
   I shall lend my ardour here!
   That their Saviour in this place
   They'll approach and have no fear.

St Thérèse of Lisieux
Extract from The Angels at the Crib
Collected Poems of St Thérèse of Lisieux
(Gracewing, England)
Translated by Alan Bancroft

References

Acknowledgements

Illustrations, Credits and Sources

Bibliography

Index of Authors

Reviews

ACKNOWLEDGEMENTS

Grateful acknowledgement is made to the following for their kind permission to reprint extracts from their works:-

ɸ   *L'Osservatore Romano* English edition, Vatican City: excerpts from weekly edition 1979-1999.

ɸ   St Pauls, UK: *Hymns to Christ,* edit. Costante Berselli, trans. Sister Mary of Jesus, O.D.C., 1982.

ɸ   St Pauls Publications, Strathfield, Australia:
    - Extracts from English translation of *Catechism of the Catholic Church* for Australia © 1994, St Pauls Publications/Libreria Editrice Vaticana. Used with permission.
    - Extracts from *Devotions to St Joseph,* 1977 and *Prayer for Holy Communion,* 1978, Fr. Brian Moore, S.J.

ɸ   United States Catholic Conference, Washington, D.C. extracts from *Catechism of the Catholic Church.* Used with permission.

ɸ   Catholic Truth Society, London: Extract from *The Credo of the People of God*, Pope Paul VI © 1968.

ɸ   Burns and Oates, Great Britain: Extracts from *The Window in The Wall,* R.A. Knox, 1956. Used with permission.

ɸ   Institute of Carmelite Studies, Washington, D.C.
    From *The Complete Works of Elizabeth of the Trinity,* Volume One, trans. by Sr. Aletheia Kane, O.C.D, copyright © 1984 by Washington Province of Discalced Carmelites, Inc, ICS Publications 2131, Lincoln Road, N.E. Washington, DC, USA.

ɸ   Sophia Institute Press, Box 5284, Manchester NHO3108, USA: from *I Believe in Love,* Père Jean du Coeur de Jésus D'Elbée, © 1974, translation of "Croire à L'Amour" by Teichert & Stebbins, Distributed in Australia by Charles Paine Ltd.

ɸ   Gracewing Ltd, 2 Southern Avenue, Leominster HR6 OQF, England, UK, for extracts from *Collected Poems of St Thérèse of Lisieux,* 2001, ISBN 0 85244 547 4, translated by Alan Bancroft.

ɸ   Tan Books & Publishers, Inc. Illinois:
- from *Thoughts of St Thérèse,* Reprinted by Tan Books & Publications, 1988.
- from *Thoughts of the Curé of Ars,* Reprinted by Tan Books & Publications, 1984.

ɸ   Secretariado dos Pastorinhos, Vice-Postulação de Francisco e Jacinta Marto, Fatima: from *Fatima in Lucia's Own Words,* edited by Fr. Kondor, svd.

ɸ   Scepter Press, USA, St Josemariá Escrivá.
-*Christ is Passing By,* 1973
-*The Way,* 1975

ɸ   Office of the Postulation of the Cause of Mother Teresa, from *Loving Jesus,* Mother Teresa. Used with permission.

ɸ   The Random House Group Ltd © the Estate of Eleanor Hull: Be Thou My Vision, from *The Poem Book of the Gael,* translated by M.E. Byrne and edited by Eleanor Hull. Originally published by Chatto & Windus. Reprinted by permission.

ɸ   Congregation of Marians of the Immaculate Conception, Stockbridge, MA. 01263 USA. Diary, St Maria Faustina Kowalska, *Divine Mercy in my Soul.* © 1987. All rights reserved. Used with permission.

ϕ   Goodwill Publishers, Inc, North Carolina: from Manual of Prayers in *The Holy Bible,* Catholic Action Edition, 1961.

ϕ   Templegate Publishers, Illinois (www.templegate.com) *The English Prayers of Sir Thomas More,* edited by Phillip Hallett, 1995.

ϕ   New City Press: Lubich, Chiara, *The Eucharist,* in *A Call to Love, Spiritual Writings, Volume I* translated by Hugh Moran, Hyde Park, © 1989.

ϕ   Libreria Editrice Vaticana 00120 Città del Vaticano: from *The Pope's Family Prayer Book,* Pope Paul VI, © 1976.

ϕ   Division of Christian Education of the National Council of the Churches of Christ in the U.S.A: Scripture quotations from *The Revised Standard Version of the Bible* © 1946, 1952 and 1971. Used with permission. All rights reserved.

ϕ   The Grail (England). Excerpts from *The Psalms* and the *Magnificat,* © 1963, 1986, 1993.

ϕ   International Committee on English in the Liturgy, Inc., excerpts from the English translation of *The Roman Missal* © 1973. All rights reserved. Excerpts authorised for reproduction only as printed in the U.S. Sacramentary.

ϕ   Costello Publishing Company, Inc., Northport, NY: excerpts from *Vatican Council II, Volume I, Revised Edition: The Conciliar & Post Conciliar Documents* edited by Austin Flannery, O.P. © 1998. Used by permission of the publisher. All rights reserved. No part of these excerpts may be reproduced, stored in a retrieval system, or transmitted in any form or by any means - electronic, mechanical, photocopying, recording or otherwise, without express permission of Costello Publishing Company.

Grateful acknowledgement is extended to the following for research services and assistance:-

- Veech Library, Catholic Institute of Sydney

- Sydney Archdiocesan Archives, St Mary's Cathedral, Sydney

- Mannix Library, Catholic Theological College, Melbourne

- State Library of New South Wales, Sydney

ILLUSTRATIONS, CREDITS AND SOURCES

Every reasonable attempt has been made to access sources and seek approval to reproduce texts, pictures and photographs. We apologise for any omissions in this regard.

p.5	Pope John Paul II with Monstrance, L'Osservatore Romano Servizio Fotografico, Vatican City. Used with permission.
p.7	Ad majorem Dei gloria, *Missale Romanum,* Ratisbonae, Belgium, 1904, Friedrich Pustet.
p.12	Angels in Adoration, Ibid, 1894.
p.14	The Agony in the Garden, *Missale Romanum,* Benziger Brothers, Inc, USA, 1944.
pp.44-45	Instruments of the Passion, *Missale Romanum,* Ratisbonae, Belgium, 1894, Friedrich Pustet.
p.56	Eucharistic Procession, Ibid, 1904.
p.76	The Crucifixion with Mary, John and Mary Magdalene, *The Treasury of the Sacred Heart,* Brepols' Catholic Press, Belgium, 1951.
p.78	Last Supper, *Canon Missae,* Domus Editorialis Marietti, Romæ, 1940.
p.88	The Pope at the Elevation of the Host, L'Osservatore Romano Servizio Fotografico, Vatican City. *L'Osservatore Romano English edition,* July 8, 1998. Used with permission.
p.96	"This is the Chalice of My Blood" *The Treasury of the Sacred Heart,* Brepols' Catholic Press, Belgium, 1951.

p.100	Chalice and Host, *Missale S. Ordini Prædicatorum,* Romæ 1933.
p.105	Paschal Lamb, *Missale Romanum,* Ratisbonae, Belgium, 1894, Friedrich Pustet.
p.110	St. Joseph, *Missale S. Ordinis Prædicatorum,* Romæ 1933.
p.120	The Crucifixion, *Missale Romanum,* Ratisbonae, Belgium, 1899, Friedrich Pustet.
p.124	Our Lord gives Himself in Holy Communion, *The Treasury of the Sacred Heart,* Brepols' Catholic Press, Belgium, 1923.
p.128	The Blessed Trinity, Ibid.
p.137	The Sacred Heart, *Missale Romanum,* Ratisbonae, Belgium, 1894, Friedrich Pustet.
p.140	Christ and the Apostles at Emmaus, *Missale S. Ordinis Prædicatorum,* Romæ 1933.
p.154	The Lord washes the feet of the Apostles, *Missale Romanum,* Ratisbonae, Belgium, 1899, Friedrich Pustet.
p.159	Christ carries His Cross, *Cantus Passionis,* Ratisbonae, Romæ, Belgium, 1918, Friedrich Pustet.
p.164	The Resurrected Christ with Mary Magdalene, *Missale Romanum,* Ratisbonae, Belgium, 1894, Friedrich Pustet.
p.166	The Ascension, Ibid.

p.178	Jesus, the Friend of Children, designed by James McCarthy.
p.180	The Good Shepherd, *The Small Roman Missal,* Pellegrini & Co, Sydney, 1931.
p.184	Adoration, *Breviarium Romanum,* Typis Polyglottis Vaticanis, 1956.
p.185	The Celebration of Mass, *Missale Romanum,* Ratisbonae, Belgium, 1944, Friedrich Pustet.
p.186	He who eats My Flesh and drinks My Blood will have eternal life, *The Small Roman Missale,* Pellegrini & Co, Sydney, 1931.
p.188	Do this in memory of Me, *The Treasury of the Sacred Heart,* Brepols' Catholic Press, Belgium, 1951.
p.190	Chalice and Sacred Host, *The Small Roman Missale,* Pellegrini & Co, Sydney, 1931.
p.192	The Holy Family, *Missale Romanum,* Ratisbonae, Belgium, 1899, Friedrich Pustet.
p.194	The Holy Face from the Shroud of Turin, painted by Sister Geneviève, © Office Central de Lisieux. Used with permission.
p.196	Angels in Prayer before the Crucifix, *Canon Missae,* Domus Editorialis Marietti, Romæ, 1940
p.198	A young girl prepares to receive her First Holy Communion from the Holy Father in Mexico, Jan. 1999, L'Osservatore Romano Servizio Fotografico, Vatican City. Used with permission.

p.199	Decorated Cross, *Missale Romanum,* Ratisbonae, Belgium, 1899, Friedrich Pustet.
p.204	The Assumption of Our Lady, Ibid.
p.205	Cross with vine leaves, Ibid.
p.208	Our Lady and St John at the foot of the Cross, *Missale S. Ordinis Prædicatorum,,* Romæ 1933.
p.212	The Annunciation, *Missale Romanum,* Ratisbonae, Belgium, 1899, Friedrich Pustet.
p.216	The Virgin Orans (The Virgin praying), (c. 1224) *The Art of the Icon,* by Iain Zaczek, published by Studio Editions, London, 1994. Reprinted by permission of The Random House Group Ltd.
p.222	Pentecost, *Missale Romanum,* Ratisbonae, Belgium, 1894, Friedrich Pustet.
p.226	I will go to the Altar of God, *Missale S. Ordinis Prædicatorum,* Romæ 1933.
p.237	Men awaiting Ordination in Rome, L'Osservatore Romano Servizio Fotografico, Vatican City. *L'Osservatore Romano English edition,* April 28, 1999. Used with permission.
p.241	Pope John Paul II lays hands at Ordination, Ibid.
p.247	Pope John Paul II speaks with Carmelite nuns in Cuba, Ibid.
p.250	Angel incensing the monstrance, *Missale Romanum,* Ratisbonae, Belgium, 1899, Friedrich Pustet.

p.290	Peace be with you, Missale Romanum, Ratisbonae 1894, Freidrich Pustet
p.300	Thanks be to God, *Missale Romanum,* Ratisbonae, Belgium, 1894, Friedrich Pustet.

BIBLIOGRAPHY

St Alphonsus Liguori, *The Holy Eucharist*, edited by Rev. Eugene Grimm, Redemptorist Fathers, U.S.A, 1934.

Ancient Devotions for Holy Communion, from Eastern and Western Sources, compiled by S.A.C., Kegan Paul, Trench, Trübner & Co. Ltd., London, 1905.

St Anthony's Treasury, A Manual of Devotions, Pellegrini & Co., Sydney, 1937. Publishers, New York, 1948.

Bernadot, M.V., O.P. *From Holy Communion to the Blessed Trinity*, translated by Dom Francis Izaard, O.S.B., Sands & Co., London, 1934.

St Augustine, *The Confessions of St Augustine, Basic Writings of St Augustine*, Vol. 1, Random House rd, O.S.B., Sands & Co., London, 1934.

Boylan, M. Eugene, O. Cist. R. *This Tremendous Love,*.
The Newman Press, Westminster, Marylands, 1962 © 1947.

Catechism of the Catholic Church, English translation, St. Pauls, Australia, 1994.

St Catherine of Siena, *The Dialogue of the Seraphic Virgin*, translated by Algar Thorold, Kegan Paul, Trench, Trübner & Co. Ltd. London, 1907.

Chautard, Dom Jean-Baptiste, *The Soul of the Apostolate*, translated by a Monk of Our Lady of Gethsemani, Abbey of Gethsemani Inc. Trappist, Kentucky, 1946.

The Divine Office, The Liturgy of the Hours according to the Roman Rite. E.J. Dwyer, Sydney, 1974.

The Documents of Vatican II, edited by Austin Flannery, O.P., Costello Publishing Co., New York, 1975

Elizabeth of the Trinity, The Complete Works, translated by Sister Aletheia Kane, O.C.D., ICS Publications, U.S.A., 1984.

Elliott, Rev. P.J., *Prayers for Receiving the Eucharist*, ACTS, Melbourne, 1981.

The English Prayers of Sir Thomas More, 1534, edited by Philip Hallett, Templegate Publishers, Illinois, 1995.

Eucharistic Hours, compiled by Most Rev. Dr. Ryan, C.M., Bishop of Sale, Pellegrini & Co. Pty. Ltd, Sydney, 1939.

Eymard, St Peter Julian,
- *A Eucharist Handbook*, Emmanuel Publications, Ohio, 1948.
- *Holy Communion*, translated by Clara Rumball, Emmanuel Publications, Ohio, 1940.
- *Our Lady of the Blessed Sacrament*, Emmanuel Publications, Ohio, 1930.
- *The Real Presence, Eucharistic Meditations*, Congregation of the Blessed Sacrament, Emmanuel Publications, Ohio, 1938.

Faber, Frederick, *The Blessed Sacrament*, Burns & Oates, London, 1861.

Fatima in Lucia's Own Words, edited by Louis Kondor, SVD, translated by Dominican Nuns of Perpetual Rosary, Postulation Centre, Fatima, Portugal, 1995.

The Holy Bible, Revised Standard Version, Collins, New York, 1973.

Hymns to Christ, edited by Costante Berselli, translated by Sister Mary of Jesus, O.D.C., St Paul Publications, Great Britain, 1982.

St Josemariá Escrivá,
- *Christ is Passing By,* Scepter Press, USA, 1973.
- *The Way,* Scepter Press, USA, 1975.

Key of Heaven, A Manual of Catholic Devotions, edited by Rev. J. Lelen. Catholic Book Publishing Co., U.S.A. and Canada, 1939.

Knox, Ronald A., *The Window in the Wall, and other Sermons on the Holy Eucharist,* Burns & Oates, London, 1956.

Laurence, Rev. Fr., O.D.C., *Golden Hours Before the Blessed Sacrament,* Mahon's Printing Works, Dublin, 1935.

L'Osservatore Romano, English edition. Vatican City, 1978-1999.

Louise de Marillac, *Prier avec Louise de Marillac,* edited by E. Charpy, Editions du Signe, Strasbourg, 1995.

Lubich, Chiara, *The Eucharist,* in *A Call to Love, Spiritual Writings, Volume I,* translated by Hugh Moran, Hyde Park, New City Press, © 1989.

McKey, Rev. Fr. J., *The Light of Other Days. Fond Memories Around Me,* David Lee and Associates, Stanthorpe, Queensland, undated.

St Margaret Mary Alacoque, *Letters,* translated by Clarence A. Herbst SJ, Henry Regnery Company, Chicago, 1954

St Maria Faustina Kowalska, *Divine Mercy In My Soul*, Marian Press, Massachusetts, 1990.

Marmion, Dom Columba, O.S.B., *Christ in His Mysteries*, translated by Mother M. St Thomas of Tyburn Convent, Sands & Co., London, 1939.

The Missal for Sundays, Brepols Turnhout, Belgium, 1936.

Missale S. Ordinis Prædicatorum auctoritate Apostolica approbatum et Reverendissimi Patris Fr. Martini Stanislai Gillet. Romæ 1933.

Missale Romanum S. Pii v. Pontificis Maximi Sumptibus, Chartis et Typis Friderici Pustet. Ratisbonae, Neo Eboraci et Cincinnati, 1894.

Moore, Fr. Brian, S.J.,
- *Devotions to St. Joseph,* St. Pauls Publications, Strathfield, 1977.
- *Prayers for Holy Communion,* St Pauls Publications, Strathfield, 1978.

Newman, John Henry, Cardinal,
- *Callista*, Burns & Oates, London, 1856.
- *Loss and Gain,* Burns & Oates, London, 1909.
- *Meditations and Devotions*, Longmans, Green & Co., London, 1893.
- *Certain Difficulties Felt by Anglicans in Catholic Teaching,* Vol. II, Longmans, Green & Co., New York, 1914.

O'Connor, James, *The Hidden Manna*, A Theology of the Eucharist, Ignatius Press, San Francisco, 1988.

One with Jesus, translated by Paul de Jaegher, S.J., Burns Oates & Washbourne Ltd., London, 1947.

Père Jean du Coeur de Jésus D'Elbée, *I Believe in Love*, translation of "Croire à l'Amour" by Teichert and Stebbins, St Bede's Publications, Massachusetts, 1974.

Plus, Raoul, S.J.,
- *God Within Us*, translated by Edith Cowell, Burns Oates & Washbourne, London, 1929.
- *In Christ Jesus*, Burns Oates & Washbourne, London, 1928.

Pope John Paul II
- *Ecclesia de Eucharistia*, Encyclical Letter, Rome 2003.
- *The Holy Eucharist*, Letter of the Supreme Pontiff on the Mystery and Worship of the Holy Eucharist, 1980, Catholic Truth Society, London.

Pope Leo XIII, *Mirae Caritatis, The Most Holy Eucharist*, Encyclical Letter, 1902, ACTS Publications, Melbourne.

Pope Paul VI
- *The Credo of the People of God*, 1968, Catholic Truth Society, London.
- *Mysterium Fidei, Mystery of Faith*, Encyclical Letter, 1965, St Paul Publications, Sydney.
- *The Pope's Family Prayer Book* translated by Mgr. Peter Coughlan, E.J. Dwyer, Sydney, 1976.

Pope Pius XII
- *Mediator Dei, Christian Worship on the Sacred Liturgy*, Encyclical Letter, 1947, Catholic Truth Society, London.
- *Mystici Corporis Christi, The Mystical Body of Jesus Christ*, Encyclical Letter, 1943, Catholic Truth Society, London.

Prayers from the Eastern Liturgies, compiled by Donald Attwater, Burns Oates & Washbourne Ltd., London, 1931.

The Psalms, The Grail, Collins, London, 1963.

Putz, J, S.J., *My Mass*, Douglas Organ, London, 1947.

The Bread of Life, arranged by H.A. Rawes, D.D., Burns & Oates, London, c.1879.

The Raccolta, Prayers and Devotions Enriched with Indulgences, Rev. J. Christopher and Very Rev. C. Spence, Benziger Brothers, U.S.A., 1944.

The Roman Missal, official English texts, E.J. Dwyer, Sydney, 1975.

The Small Roman Missal, Pellegrini, Sydney, 1931.

Teresa, Mother, *Loving Jesus*, translated by Susana Labastida. Harper Collins Publishers, London, 1991.

St. Thérèse of Lisieux,
- *Collected Poems of St.Thérèse of Lisieux,* translated by Alan Bancroft, ISBN 0 85244 574 4, Gracewing Ltd, 2 Southern Avenue, Leominster HR6 OQF, England, UK, 2001.
- Poésies, Editions du Cerf/Desclée de Brouwer, 1979.
- *Thoughts of St Thérèse,* translation from "Pensées" by an Irish Carmelite, Tan Books & Publishers, U.S.A. © 1915, P.J. Kennedy & Sons.

Thibaut, Dom Raymond, *Union with God*, according to the letters of direction of Dom Marmion, translated by Mother Mary St. Thomas, Sands & Co., London, 1949.

Thomas à Kempis, *The Imitation of Christ*, revised translation based upon Bishop Challoner's text 1737, Burns, Oates & Washbourne, Great Britain, 1915.

St Thomas Aquinas
- *Summa Theologiae*, Marietti, Rome, 1948.
- *Summa Theologica*, translated by Fathers of the English Dominican Province, Benziger Brothers, U.S.A. 1947.

The Treasury of the Sacred Heart, Brepols' Catholic Press, Belgium, 1923.

von Hildebrand, Dietrich, *Liturgy and Personality,* Longmans, Green & Co., New York, 1943.

The Worship of the Eucharist, Incorporated Catholic Truth Society, compiled by Stephen Dean, London, 1981.

INDEX OF AUTHORS

St Alphonsus Liguori (1696-1787), 17, 168, 174.

St Ambrose (340-397), 108-109.

St Augustine of Hippo (354-430), 25, 97, 151.

St Basil (329-379), 135.

St Bonaventure (1221-1274), 43.

Boylan, Eugene (1904-1964), 40.

Caswall, Edward (1814-1878), 74.

St Catherine of Siena (1347-1380), 107, 173.

Chaucer, Geoffrey (c.1340-1400), 219.

Cosmas of Maiuma (d. c.770), 131.

Chautard, Dom Abbot Jean Baptiste (1858-1935), 49, 229, 243.

Damien de Veuster, Blessed (1840-1889), 31.

d'Elbée, Père Jean du Coeur de Jésus 122, 138, 206.

Donne, John (1572-1631), 51.

Elizabeth of The Trinity, Blessed (1880-1906), 139, 279.

St Ephrem of Syria (c.307-373), 44-45, 167.

Faber, Fr. Frederick (1814-1863), 54, 213.

St Gertrude (1256-1301), 171.

St Gregory of Narek (951-1003), 161.

Hagspiel, Bruno SVD (1885-1961), 233.

Hildebrand, Dietrich von (1889-1977), 40.

Hopkins, Gerard Manley SJ (1844-1889), 53, 69.

Hull, Eleanor Henrietta (1860-1935), 52.

St Ignatius of Antioch (d.107), 40.

Innocent VI, Pope (1282-1362), 209.

St John Chrysostom (c.347-407), 48.

John Paul II, Pope (b. 1920), 5, 12, 26, 27, 28, 34, 36, 40, 48, 80-81, 84-85, 92, 93, 94, 102, 112, 132, 140, 148, 170, 181, 199-205, 209, 214, 217, 218, 220, 226, 228, 230, 232, 234-235, 236,238, 240, 246, 248, 258, 268.

St John Vianney (1786-1859), 31, 138, 146, 170, 176, 232.

St Josemariá Escrivá de Balaguer (1902-1975), 30, 31, 50.

Knox, Mgr. Ronald (1888-1957), 130, 132.

St Louise de Marillac (1591-1660), 114-115.

Lubich, Chiara (b.1920), 102.

St Margaret Mary Alacoque (1647-1690), 136.

St Maria Faustina Kowalska (1905-1938), 96, 278.

Marmion, Abbot Joseph Columba, Blessed (1858-1923), 104, 106.

Merry del Val, Cardinal Raphael (1865-1930), 115.

Moore, Brian SJ (1931-1997), 111, 223.

Mother Teresa (1910-1997), 91, 232, 259, 268.

Newman, Cardinal John Henry (1801-1890), 19, 82, 100, 125, 142, 210, 213, 218.

Paul VI, Pope (1897-1978), 27, 86-87, 186.

St Peter Julian Eymard (1811-1868), 93, 138, 146,220.

Pius XII, Pope (1876-1958), 46, 112, 118, 150, 152.

Plus, Raoul SJ (1882-1958), 139.

Putz, Joseph SJ (b.1894), 126.

Ryan, C.M. Bishop Patrick John , 19.

Stanfield, Francis (1835-1914), 61.

St Thérèse of Lisieux (1873-1897), 32-33, 141, 142, 176, 184, 280.

Thomas à Kempis (1379-1471), 46, 242, 244, 245

St Thomas Aquinas (1224-1274), 58, 64, 66, 68, 77, 95, 97, 101, 116, 127, 143-145, 156-157, 170.

St Thomas More (c.1469-1535), 105, 171.

REVIEW

Our Lord in the Gospel (Mt 13:52) speaks of *"the householder who brings out of his treasure new things and old."*

In this impressive collection of *"Prayers and Meditations for Eucharistic Adoration"* the editor has done exactly that: extracts from recent conciliar documents and papal Exhortations are framed between instances of Eucharistic piety from all ages and many rites. Doctrine and devotion here find harmonious expressions. As Pope John Paul has said, faith should proceed simultaneously from the heart and mind. Here that ideal is manifestly achieved.

This booklet will serve as support and inspiration to Eucharistic devotion and no aim can be higher or more useful than to assist believers to focus their minds and hearts on what is the nerve-centre of the Catholic faith, namely belief in the miracle of the abiding Real Presence of Christ Our Lord among us in the Blessed Sacrament.

Brother Christian Moe FSC
St Bede's College, Mentone